No Aloha

No Aloha

THE FRIENDLY HAPPY
MUSIC OF THE PAST

Deran Ludd

Semiotext(e) / Smart Art Press

This novel is dedicated to my grandmother, Dorothy Caroline Ravenscroft Owens. Special and eternal thanks are reserved for Jesse Bernstein, Katherine Francillon, Chris Kraus and Christine Strati.

Portions of this book appeared, in a slightly different form, in the following publications: More and Less, Vol. 2 #1 (Art Center College of Design) and the online zine Pug, #4 (www.pugzine.com).

This is Smart Art Press Volume VII, No. 61

ISBN: 1-58435-008-3
Book design: Ben Meyers
Author Photo: Katherine Francillon
Book design: Ben Meyers

We gratefully acknowledge financial assistance in the publication of this book from the Literature Program of the New York State Council on the Arts

Printed in the United States of America

Evening shadows make me blue,
when each weary day is through

—Connie Francis,
  "My Happiness"

And now the purple dusk of twilight-time
steals across the meadows of my heart

—Stardust

The George Baker Selection

Not-so-distant meat grinder thud and rumble of civil war. Stink of fire and gun smoke over Denver, Colorado. Gun smoke. Aftershave of the Old West, and now of the Late West.

It's the same smoke, dark and acrid, that is drifting in heavy clouds over much of North America. The smoke and fire of market-driven hyper-chaos. Accompanied by a dull slaughterhouse roar of episodic racial or cultural pogroms and low-intensity class warfare.

And oh yes, I am sure you can well imagine the shock! The United States finding itself self-destructing under a little known sunset clause in the nation's founding social compact. But...not only that!... Who would have thought! Shopping malls, hog farms and theme parks as the final heirs of this great imperial adventure game.

And that muck directly below us? The Mile High (in gore) City, Denver. Capital of that formerly beloved tourist destination, and now Christ-loving and blood-drenched land, the state of Colorado. Crossroads of the continent, and stronghold of many quaint popular End Time enthusiasms. Such as electing a televangelist as tyrant of the state on his promise of full employment through the mass murder and/or vivisection of sinners. And when the United Nations finally intervened...it was of course too late—barbarism is almost always a terminal social infection.

You don't believe me? Alright, let's go on down there.

Hugo Montenegro and His Orchestra and Chorus

Tall wide battered sign at street level, big arrow pointing to the right, above the arrow the words EMERGENCY ROOM.

Vast suburban hospital complex. Lots of groomed trees, lots of parking. Parkinglots as superterrific open-air triage extravaganza. The dead and wounded fresh this very minute. Dead and wounded spilling out further and further from the previously tastefully decorated ER entrance.

Dazed medicals trying to keep the injured lined in rows on one side and tagged with a piece of white plastic, each has a different black number hurriedly stenciled on it. And trying to keep the dead piled to the other side and tagged with a stenciled white number on a black plastic tag.

And the moaning and the crying. Loud, desperate and angry voices are all around, wherever you are. Running, running everywhere.

Medicals in gore-smeared blues and whites. People bleeding and bleeding and more and more blood and viscera that decontamination teams no longer even pretend to clean up. Ad hoc triage squads. Weary dissolute teams of corpse removers.

The dying and injured, and the numbed and shocked survivors, are all the standard variety of woman and man and child in any late-20th-Century suburb.

A few-dozen uniformed soldiers from the Golden West (the mall republic the Euros call it) are off in one corner doing nothing. The Westerners' raggedy-assed banner—horizontal blue band over a horizontal green band and a golden sunrise with eleven rays jutting up—is the only real sign of their claimed authority in Colorado. Or, what used to be Colorado.

Colorado: from ski resort and winter wonderland to bloody religious vortex in just a few short years. Not so hard to understand. Because once Out West seceded, and Back East splintered, it was just a hop, skip and a jump to the S&P 500 shifting their capital out and about and wait and see. And that was that. Without consumerism to distract the North Americans, religious fundamentalism was their only remaining national trait. And God without shopping, as usual, led to fire and carnage.

It was in the latter days of Ronald Reagan's seventh presidential term. The penultimate Nancy years—when chief sadist and First-Lady-for-Life Nancy and her personal gestapo, the Drug Enforcement Administration, really ran the United States.

This was the continental mood that opened the floodgates and swept televangelist Bill Kingson into the Colorado governor's mansion. Kingson and his campaign promises (fulfilled!) to defeat Satan and wipe out the state's unemployment via the Surgical Jesus Mind Project.

It is the small unit of a couple-dozen Blue Helmets (mostly Mexican and Euro)—clerks and soldiers of the United Nations' North American Arbitration (UNNAA)—that are trying to manage the flood of vehicles, the dead and the wounded, and the numbed and shocked survivors. Mandated by the Security Council to help reconstitute a viable United States, UNNAA was never significantly funded, never really more than a moral palliative for the remaining world powers.

Sure UNNAA got dictator Kingson to leave Colorado, but with no successor government ready to step in to the vacuum, it hadn't been more than a day after Kingson fled that his lieutenants began battling over the remains of Colorado. That chaos lasted several months before the international community moved in and tried to restore sanity and humanity to the state. But the sanity didn't take, and neither did the post-Kingson cease-fire mediated for UNNAA by retired South African President Nelson Mandela.

The late-September thunder and lightening barely marks mention beside the more intimate horror storm of explosion and fire rippling the nighttime horizon to the south of the medical complex. The grunting artillery and rocket salvos pummeling Denver's southern suburbs. Tossing globs of death up and over. Here and there. The steadily inclement weather of civil war.

Sirens strobing, horn blaring, a big six-wheel EMS truck careens through shrubs, barricade sawhorses, plows between cars heading full-bore for the ER entrance. Injured and medicals thrown this way and that. The EMS truck comes to a screaming halt that spins the big ambulance in an arc ending with the backdoors facing the ER entrance. Soldiers run to driver's door.

The female african american driver is dead. Long dead. Strapped in by her seatbelt, leaning back against the blood-washed seat. Two bloody clotted bullet holes in her chest.

666King scrawled in blood on the windshield.

The soldiers run to the back of the vehicle just as a hispanic medical yanks open the double doors.

Red red. Sure, after what? Six months of desolate siege? Any ambulance is bound to be encrusted with viscera and blood. But, when you look inside this vehicle…there is initial vertigo—the entire inside of the ambulance is coated on

10

all the visible surfaces in blood and the eviscerated bits and remains of whatever—impossible to orient the brain to what the eyes are seeing.

"There!"

A caucasian medical in grimy coveralls points to a human form strapped to a gurney. A dozen hands yank the gurney onto the pavement. These hands, a few still wearing degraded and torn latex gloves, sweep away the blood-caked blanket from the body of a caucasian boy, maybe 11 or 12 years old.

The boy is smeared head-to-foot with blood. The boy's blood-clotted clothing is cut away. The only external injuries are two shallow lacerations on his chest.

The torn girl clothing the boy wore—frock thing, underwear, pullover—is tossed away unnoted.

This particular triage squad has been on duty more-or-less for a week. Each of them is operating on technical know-how and large plastic barrels of meta-amphetamine tablets. Courtesy of the Golden West Pharmaceutical Manufacturer's Benevolence Roundtable.

The boy has plenty of vital signs. No sign of dying. No apparent reason for all the blood covering the boy and the inside of the ambulance.

It is at this moment that the second person in the back of the ambulance becomes known. A tall asian american man throws aside a bloodied tarp he has hidden under in the furthest back of the ambulance. A black cop, gawking in at the ambulance's bloody interior, is startled by the asian man's sudden appearance and the cop awkwardly reaches for his sidearm. Too slow, the asian gunman shoots him. The gunman in the back of the ambulance leaps out of the vehicle. As he lands the gunman points to the bloody boy on the gurney and shouts:

"This boy is the Messiah! Get him help!"

The gunman carries a .45 caliber semiautomatic pistol with an extended clip. When no one immediately moves to help the boy the asian american gunman grabs a young caucasian american medical by the throat and presses his pistol to the medical's head.

"I'll kill the doctor!"

Weapons are raised, but one of the triagists blurts out.

"The kid's OK!…"

The asian man pauses, momentarily uncertain, and then drags his hostage to the open ER doors.

"Get the boy in here…or I'll kill the doctor!"

It is a young Mexican Blue Helmet that runs over and starts shoving at the gurney, moving it into the hospital.

Inside ER there is no waiting area, no reception, no hallways, no restrooms, no demarcated anything at all. Dead people. More than the baggers can get rid of. The wounded, and the horribly and fatally injured. The medicals try to limit the suffering of the dying and just stabilize the rest. Everywhere. And the noise, the shouting, groaning. The brutal unusual noises that scratch up along the back of the neck and tremor and nag at the brain pan.

Gore-splashed pastel walls and recessed lighting.

Man with the gun looks at the boy on the gurney and looks around and yells:

"Hurry!"

Everyone looks at each other. An older black medical steps up and uses a wet cloth to swab the boy's face until his pale slack and slightly parted lips are cleaned. The medical looks the asian american man right in the eyes. The medical turns, adjusts the kid's head, reaches into the boy's mouth to move aside his tongue, and then pinches closed the boy's small nose. Medical exhales steadily into the boy's mouth and the boy coughs and chokes. The medical turns the boy's head to the side. The kid feebly throws up.

"See? He's OK. Really, man."

A white female medical gingerly dabs at the two lacerations on the boy's chest—already cleaned and clotting.

"Those cuts aren't deep.... Look...."

The gunman leans forward some and stares at the boy. The boy on the gurney opens his eyes and feebly reaches out to the asian american man. The gunman releases the young white medical, and steps back and wipes his sweating face with the sleeve of his topcoat. He has tears in his eyes. He speaks quietly to the boy.

"My Lord, you are safe now...."

He puts the pistol's barrel deep in his own mouth, so it's pointed to the back of his skull, and pulls the trigger.

One or two people on the scene shake their heads or glance at one another. Most do not, they are all too busy. Two body baggers (one caucasian american and one hispanic american) stuff the dead man into an opaque plastivinyl bodybag.

The boy is crying, he starts to sit up on the gurney, two aides (both caucasian) flop him back down and roll the gurney toward a bank of elevators.

An older caucasian american doctor mutters and squints officiously, keying in his report to a hand-deck that is beaming a signal to the complex's in-house intranet that has not been up for over a year. Everyone ignores him as they work and suffer.

Outside, two body baggers struggle along with a heap of emptied body bags. One of the baggers, a caucasian american guy, nudges his fellow body bagger, a mixed-race guy, and then points to the bloodied girl clothing cut off the boy. The other bagger smirks.

"You wish. He's breathing. White tag. You don't touch him."

The caucasian bagger stares at the girl clothes, already lost underfoot. He stops, drops his end of the burden, dashes between two medicals and grabs up the girl underwear that has been slit at each leg to get them off the boy. The white man stuffs them deep into a coverall pocket.

Spencer Ross
and His Orchestra

The boy is only occasionally conscious for the rest of that day and night and he fakes unconsciousness into the next day. He is in a sort of dorm, crowded with cots occupied by boys with minor injuries. There are very few medicals posted here. The boys are put in a bed, sedated and periodically dosed with food and antibiotics.

Late in the day three fighter bombers, affiliated with one of ex-Pastor Governor Kingson's onetime lieutenants, now a contending regional warlord, rip through the sky above the hospital complex firing rockets scatter-shot into the open-air triage out front. The explosions and the sound barrier being triply broken shakes and shatters glass everywhere.

Two of the jets come screaming back, emptying the remainder of their rocket payload into the hospital's twin parking towers, now ad hoc surgeries and morgues. The third jet returns, and launches several rockets that explode and shower small glossy four-color pamphlets urging repentance and allegiance to a new would-be Pastor Governor.

In the wake of the attacks, and the screaming of other children, the boy slinks out of bed. He is naked except for the bandages on his chest. He winces as he stretches, pulling at the bandages. He runs out into the hall.

Sticking close to the wall the white boy slinks through the halls. In one of the rooms he finds girls his own age or so. As he enters the room, the two oldest girls (one caucasian and one black) stand up and threaten him with their fists, he glares and waves a bloodied scalpel at them. The girls step back. The boy hurriedly rifles through a closet of girl clothes. He keeps an eye on the two older girls and tightly grips the scalpel in one fist. He grabs a warm-looking pullover and red stirrup stretch pants. When he snatches the later, one of the younger girls (mixed-race american) lets out a squeak.

"Those are mine, damn it! They're...girl's!"

"Shut up. I'll stab you...."

She stares at her pants that he's stealing. The oldest girls sneaks up and takes a swing at him. Her fist connects with his head. The boy slams forward into the wall. His head bounces a bit. He is not really hurt. He grabs some lined rubber boots and underwear and two pair of socks. The older girls both approach menacingly. The white boy lurches to the room's door. He throws the scalpel, the girls scramble aside. He runs. A hispanic girl yells:

"Bastard."

She throws a drinking glass. It loudly shatters on the hall floor.

Out back of the hospital, near the mounds of hospital refuse, the boy quickly dresses in the girl clothes. On a wall of the hospital incinerator, back near the parkinglot is spray-painted *666King*. This red graffito is crossed over with the word *Zapata* spray painted in green. The blue pull-over is part wool and even so the boy is cold and the pink rubber boots are tight and they are going to hurt after awhile so the boy decides he better go fast now while he can.

Ferrante
and Teicher

The UNICEF rations are not sitting well on Gus' stomach. Very little does anymore. Gus knows he has to eat. He forces the first sandwich down, but before he can get down the second his stomach catches up. Gus' stomach throbs and he is nauseous and he swallows mouthfuls of saliva and he starts to sweat. Gus belches long and low. Don't throw up, don't throw up, just belch.

Gus looks at his second sandwich given out at the UNNAA station a few kilometers back. Kids first, the Ethiopian Blue Helmet said. Gus relaxes worry and concentration lines out of his face so he looks under-18, and qualifies for the UNICEF food. The Blue Helmet nods her head as she glances at the three kids. Five minutes later they are each clutching two Blue Plate Specials—vitamin-fortified bread, spread and grain-loaf.

Gus sits back and takes a slow deep breath. His stomach is going to take the food. Gus looks at his two companions. Gladys, chubby caucasian girl, youngest of the three, and Maude, a chubby black teenager. Gus is also caucasian, 15, 16 centimeters taller than either of the girls, and heavier.

Maude says Gus could have trained to be a sumotori, become a yokozuna maybe. But now his ill stomach, and the civil war, eat at his build.

All three kids have Red Cross-provided de-lousing buzz-cuts.

Maude and Gladys are intent on eating every crumb and slurp of their Blue Plate Specials. Gus watches them. He looks away and holds his sandwich toward them. They look at him as they chew. Maude reaches for it. Gladys is chewing a big bite of a sandwich. She makes complaining noises through her mouthful of food. She swallows enough to squawk:

"Me...too...."

Gus roughly pulls the sandwich in half and sets part on Maude's jeans leg, and starts to set the other on Gladys' leg. Gladys squawks as she chews, this time staring fearfully at the food about to touch the dirty and torn orange cotton tights she has over other layers of clothes. Gus' face twitches. He looks at Gladys. The food is still poised near her leg, but now because she's so twitchy about it. Gus sneers.

They'd stolen these tights off a girl on the train a few weeks ago. Gladys hadn't stopped wearing them since. It shows. Gladys finally swallows.

"My new tights?! Like, that's really rude, Gus. Hand it to me."

Gus shrugs and Maude laughs.

"C'mon, time to go wait for a train."

Gus stands up and belches and Gladys says:

"Let me finish eating. If I walk and eat...my stomach gets upset."

Gus belches again and shakes his head at Gladys and walks on ahead. Maude grabs up her younger friend's satchel.

"C'mon, Glad. Sooner we get to his friends', sooner we'll be inside and warm.... Probably food...right?"

Gladys sighs and jumps up.

"*Friend*? A friend, who like, pays to, like, do...stuff...to you?"

Maude gives Gladys a look.

18

"Don't give Gus any shit about Rodriguez. Right?"

"Geez, Maude. Like, I'm not saying anything Gus hasn't said…."

"Let Gus do any talking about it. Right?"

Gladys nods crankily and she stumbles. Gladys is wearing a pair of green platform shoes they stole from a woman that morning on a B3 train. The platform shoes are significantly too large for Gladys and lift her a precarious 10 centimeters beyond her own height.

"Maybe the Rodriguezes got a satellite dish? You could get us TV if they have a dish. Right?"

"If there's electricity."

"Oh, shit. Right."

Gladys shrugs and adjusts the three pairs of socks she's wearing to help fill the platform shoes. She starts off again, chewing the last of Gus' sandwich. Maude looks back. A last check. Always things are disappearing, falling away, getting lost.

Gus sees the girls haven't caught up. He shifts his satchels and touches his stomach gingerly and belches.

"Christ…. C'mon."

Maude runs to catch up and Gladys starts off fast but stumbles and curses. Gus yells at her.

"Put your fuckin' boots back on. You're wasting time."

"I had to hit that chick hard to get these…."

"I did all the hitting."

"I punched her a bunch of times!…"

"Put your fuckin' boots back on, Glad. We can tie your disco shoes onto Gus' bag…."

Gus is walking back to Gladys.

"Right, Gus? Right?"

"Whatever."

Gus holds out his arm and Gladys braces herself on it as she sheds the green platforms and returns to her walking boots. As she changes shoes, you can see her skin is a dirty gray, not pink.

Maude walks on ahead several meters. She looks down a street and spots a battered MetroWeb sign a few blocks away.

"I see a train sign down that street."

Gus grabs Gladys' left hand as she stands up and he grabs Maude's right hand and they hurry to the crossroads. There are some locals on their carports and front steps watching the three youths. Gus squints at the MetroWeb sign. He puts on his baseball cap to shade-off some of the sun. The girls already have their caps on. All three of the caps have the kid's favorite sumotori's tegata—their handprint in red and their name in black kanji characters—embroidered on the crown front. On the back of each cap, the embroidered logo of a major corporate sponsor of the beya that that wrestler belongs to.

As they approach the entrance of the light-rail MetroWeb station Gus squeezes Maude's hand and looks at the blue lettered and numbered sign over the entrance. Maude watches her partner struggle to apply what reading she's taught him.

"Letter, B. Number, Two.... N.... E...."

Gus falters on the W. Maude grins and slaps Gus on the ass.

"I told you, man."

They high-five.

"I fucking told you. Right? You're reading signs. Right?"

"But what's after the N and the E?"

Maude shakes her head.

"No."

But Gladys butts in.

"Next is a W. W. Newww.... Springfield."

20

Gladys runs ahead as Maude takes a half-hearted swing at her. Maude points to the big route map embedded in the wall of the station.

"You read the map."

"It'll take me too long…."

"I will! I'll do it."

Gladys runs up to the wall-sized and color-coordinated diagram of the Denver MetroWeb—four blue concentric circles, the four B lines, and four red axis lines, intersecting in downtown Denver, the four A lines. The two-tone grid is a colorful bomb site over the greater metro Denver region.

To the left of the enormous MetroWeb diagram there are a few tattered notices of line closures and re-routes. These pieces of paper are weathered and torn. The newest notices are dated more than a year ago. No updates, or addenda. These notices and forms, now decomposing, are a simple obit for the former United States. No funeral notice, too few mourners.

Further up the wall, beyond these remnants of official-dom, is the red painted graffito *666King*.

Acrid smoke from something nearby burning wafts through the station and out front. The kids cough and choke.

Gladys jumps and points to a station way up on the map out of reach.

"Lakewood."

She adds:

"It's a…B4 station. North of I-80."

Maude searches the southeastern section of the MetroWeb map. She points to a station a third of the way counter-clockwise from Lakewood.

"We're here…. Or, this next one…."

Gladys looks from Lakewood to their most likely present location.

"Christ, Gus, like, that's…still so far."

Gladys' young voice drains off in weary complaint.

They walk on into the platform area, this station is administered by a small Golden West Guard detachment. These Guards have decided to check the papers and possessions of everyone who wants to enter. More playing at being in charge of Colorado.

IDs to satisfy these Westerners are no problem. But they don't like Gladys' Ultra PlayDeck 8220. They threaten to break open the toy to make sure she's not smuggling. Gladys starts growling. Gus grabs her and holds her. The commotion draws the attention of a male caucasian Guard sergeant. He storms over, thinking Gus is some guy molesting child refugees.

Maude explains what's going on and shows him the proper IDs. The sergeant looks at the electronic toy, and then at Gladys, who is staring at her beloved PlayDeck.

"These…"

The sergeant shakes the electronic toy he has grabbed.

"…are part of why the United States died!"

Maude slightly smirks, luckily the soldiers do not see her.

The Westerner's eyes are bulging.

"What are you gonna do?! We don't fucking want you in the Golden West. That's for damn sure!"

No spoken answer.

"What are you gonna do? Play a fucking game?!"

Gladys keeps her eyes to the ground.

"The Blue Helmets are pulling out!"

The surprise the kids show makes the sergeant laugh.

"Mandela's cease-fire's collapsed! UNNAA's getting out of Colorado!"

Gus' face twitches. The sergeant smirks and coughs, and

then spits and says:

"The Soviets don't want you! They're only taking scientists."

The sergeant laughs harshly and tosses the game unit at the kids as he strides away. Gladys reaches out and grabs the electronic toy in mid-air. She glares after the Westerners.

"Fucking cops...."

"They're soldiers."

Gladys sneers at Gus.

"Fucking cops."

Once the Guards move on, everyone breaks ranks. The station is not too crowded. The youths move aside on their own.

There are a couple dozen Tribbers—members of another of the United States' bastard offspring; the Secret Rapture Movement, down at the other end of the platform. The core belief of the Secret Rapture being that the Original Christians were all secretly Raptured on June 11th and 13th, six years previous. Humanity is now in the midst of the Tribulation. Satan's Salad Days.

These Tribbers are en route to Dallas, of course. Dallas, Texas, for the Second Coming of Jesus Christ. Dealy Plaza. The Grassy Knoll at Dealy Plaza.

Truly fevered Tribber Christians are Repenters. Repenters are easy to spot. To symbolize that they've already heard the angelic trumpets announcing Jesus' Second Coming in Dallas, Texas, the Repenters cut their own ears off. They also wear a sash of white opaque plastic from their left shoulder down to their right hip. The sashes have lists on them. Lists of names. Lists of different lengths. The names are hand lettered. The names are those of sinners, who, unwilling to concede the Living Presence of Jesus, were dispatched to the Last Four Things.

23

Gus spots a row of payphones that look functional. He reaches over and touches Gladys' shoulder and nods toward the phones. Gladys scowls.

"Like, *I* cracked the number for the card. But, like, *you're* using it up."

Gus shakes his head a little. Gladys glares.

"I could only get 2 hours credit on to it…."

Gus just looks at her. His face solid and blank. Gladys looks at Maude. Maude avoids them both and eases to a crouch among their possessions. She lights a slender handrolled cig.

"I'll watch your stuff, Glad…."

"Fuck. Alright."

Gladys swivels and trots toward the payphones. A stride or two and Gus catches up with her.

"I never use more'n a few seconds each call…."

Gladys irritatedly cuts him off.

"The card pays out by the minute…."

After they find a payphone with dialtone and a functional card slot, Gladys reaches into her layered clothes and finds the two hard plastic cards. Gus covers her from behind and to one side. Making sure no one's moving in.

Gladys picks up the handset, rests it between her shoulder and chin and then presses 0 three times. Immediately following the initial tone Gladys inserts her black jack card and waits a moment while the card flim-flams the telecom system. After she hears the second tone she removes the first card and quickly inserts the phonecard she's boosted. Most of the time payphones will take the phonecard as valid.

It works and Gladys hears the third tone and she holds out the handset to Gus who grabs it and keys in the comforting telephone number.

Gus listens to the phone rings and then the voicemail answers. He listens to Calvin Rodriguez's voice recite a

24

simple phrase. Gus hangs up, turns and walks away.

"See…only a second…."

Gladys ignores him and says:

"A train…."

They run over to Maude, who also hears the train. She has already shouldered her satchel.

Gus leads, plowing a path through people to the platform edge. Near where the end of the train will probably stop. When they want to rob passengers the kids try to entrain on the last car and work their way forward.

In a few minutes they have squeezed aboard one of the last of this mismatched string of commuter and freight cars.

Gus wants to move on, Gladys and Maude want to sit awhile. This rear car has most of its windows and the entire ceiling and it really is warm and dry. Pleasant even. If you ignore the latrinish stench. Gus looks around.

"OK. Ten minutes."

Gladys smirks and plucks out a small and slender plastic digital clock.

"Like, how are *you* gonna know when it's ten minutes?…"

Gus ignores her and takes three leisurely puffs on a cigarette butt. He stands up, last of the butt between thumb and forefinger.

"OK. Let's go. *Now.*"

"Fuck you, Gus…."

Maude stands up and swings at Gladys.

"Thanks, Gladys."

Gladys dodges most of the blow. She and Maude follow Gus.

There's no one quite right for robbery on this train. The youths never try robbery when just their fists aren't enough

25

to get what they want and get away safe. Train pulls into a station and Gus steps into an opening door and wedges his big booted foot so the doors won't close.

Maude heads through the forced open doorway, but Gladys complains:

"It's like, too fucking cold…."

"There's nothing on this train."

"Maude…. C'mon. You're cold too."

"We gotta get some money. Right?"

"Shit."

Gus grips Gladys' shoulder and pulls her out onto the platform. She stumbles a bit and glares at Gus.

"Sometime I'm gonna stay on the train…."

"Uh-huh."

Gus steps out onto the platform. It is a cold rainy day. This station is mostly rubble. Somewhere along the last few years this station was wasted by fire and mob. Stink of scorched concrete and decomposing whatever. No roof or walls to speak of. A few other people have exited the train and are standing around. There are a few makeshift shelters in the station built of scraps and rubble.

Toward the other end of the station platform there's a squad of Golden West Guards, their banner limp and damp. These soldiers are more intent on the dry spot they've encamped in than on the travelers and refugees milling around what is now an open-air amphitheater of ruins. There's not enough of them to do anything and just enough to draw the ire of the restless and worse-off refugees.

The kids make their way to some overhanging trees. A little shelter from the rain while waiting for another train.

The three youths start to unshoulder their satchels when suddenly there are screams. The crowd starts mobbing in fear. The panic in the station is tempoed by the increasingly loud dangerous cruel barking shouts of young male voices. Louder and louder. The barking chant over and over.

"Jesus! Jesus! Jesus!…"

Gladys turns to run, Maude grabs her. Gus crouches with his dagger out. Maude yanks his arm.

"We can't fight 'em! Come on!"

Maude, gripping Gladys' hand, runs through the wrecked doorway of a men's restroom.

A pack of Team Jesus paramilitaries charge down onto the platform. Carrying club crucifixes fashioned from iron bars welded together.

Pastor Governor Kingson's Team Jesus is sort of a theocratic police-state pyramid scheme, self-help death squad extortion racket for white people. Believers of color? No shortage! And plenty of dutiful women! There always are.

UNNAA dismantled the Surgical Jesus Mind Project sites that the mobs hadn't destroyed as soon as they arrived in Colorado. But the Blue Helmets never got secure enough on the ground in Colorado to disarm Team Jesus. For a short while, just after Kingson went into exile, they were not in the streets and many had renounced their previous membership. But the real Team players secreted themselves down in their bunkers, swarmed around their leaders and bosses. Now, as the Johannesburg Ceasefire is unraveling and UNNAA pulls out…. Team Jesus' bloodied iron crucifixes are making a popular comeback. Even though they supported none of the post-Kingson claimants to authority in Colorado, Team Jesus was already busy, busy, busy. There may be no more Project sites to run, but there is always Jesus' work to be done. Sinners to be sent on to fiery Gehenna.

The restroom's exterior wall is smashed outward. Gus and Maude toss Gladys up and she catapults over the rubble.

27

Maude starts up after her, but some of the rubble comes loose, and she slides back. Gus scoops his finger-entwined hands under Maude's right foot and Maude makes it over the top. Gus flings himself after her.

After Gus lands, the volume of screaming back in the station increases and small-arms fire is heard. Gus smirks. With the Blue Helmets' rapid evacuation of Colorado, the Westerners are the only government-like thing left on the ground, and so the Guards, usually draftees, bear the brunt of it all. The Westerners in this station are in no mood for God's boys.

Not far from the MetroWeb station the neighborhood disintegrates right down to burnt and melted building shells and assorted rubble. The kids have to pick their way more carefully among the stinking ruins. Maude scowls and sniffs.

"Jesus. Burnt plastics is the worst."

Gladys shakes her head no, and through mouth and nose covered by a piece of bright blue shawl she says:

"Dead people are the worst."

"Burnt plastic."

"Burnt dead things."

Gus shoves at Maude. She stumbles, recovers and then punches Gus. He ignores her and says:

"That all you two got to talk about? Then shut up."

The three teens head off toward the darkness of a hill rising ahead of them.

Burt Bacharach and His Orchestra and Chorus

The youths cross through ruins of a public school and through semi-occupied residential-multiplex enclaves.

They come to remnants of a tall chainlink fence. After some woods there is another line of destroyed chainlink fence. Woods end in fields that a couple years ago were sweeping manicured lawns. Landscaping and gardening now invisible.

It is dark now. Rain showers have ended, the wind picks up and moves the clouds out of sight. Everything is wet and sharply cold. In the night sky the brightest stars and a couple human-made satellites glitter. The largest objects overhead are two geosynchronous billboard platforms up in the stratosphere. Currently unlit, their vast 5-by-10 kilometer ultra-thin LCD screens are retracted. The billboards are passing silently overhead toward stationary orbits above Central America for an upcoming laundry detergent ad campaign.

Gladys, Gus and Maude stand at the woods' edge. Before them is an open field. The savaged ruins of a large psychiatric hospital lay out beyond the field. The kids scrutinize the much-overgrown and shadowy complex as best they can, up and down the rows of mostly wrecked and burnt buildings. No overt signs of current human occupation. Only birds and small animals in residence.

The kids stick to the trees and circle the weed-filled structures. They creep across the field, toward a few intact buildings.

Following the wall of one of the buildings the kids pick their way through underbrush and brambles. Remnants of sidewalks, now tossed and heaved, an impediment to their transit. They arrive at a more open area, what had been the main entrance to this facility. Gaping holes in the structure indicating fiery explosions. Gus points his small flashlight in through a couple of the gaps and scrutinizes the dark smelly interior.

Along an exterior wall is a large burnished steel sign. Nearly broken from all its mountings, the lower right corner of the sign leans on the ground. Scars and dings from heavy-caliber machinegun fire. Graffiti, slogans and tags are messed across its surface. The biggest and clearest graffito is *666King*, way up the wall where the sign is still sort of attached.

If you stand back a short distance, sort of where the kids are, there beneath all the scarrage and defacing, the big black enameled lettering engraved deep into the sheet of steel is still very clear. Gus holds his flashlight beam on the big familiar psychiatric symbol overlaid on a crucifix, next to words he cannot read.

The big block lettering states: COLORADO SURGICAL JESUS MIND CENTER, NO. 14. BY THE AUTHORITY OF THE NAME OF JESUS, OVER ALL THE WORKS OF SATAN. GRANTED ON THIS DAY, TO THE CITIZEN BELIEVERS OF CHRISTIAN COLORADO. PASTOR GOVERNOR BILL KINGSON.

The economically desperate and biblically deranged citizens of Colorado elected Bill Kingson by a landslide. And the plebiscites in the immediate post-landslide period that made him Pastor Governor, and made abortion and homosexuality capital felonies, among other Tough Love legislation, were swept through with mandating electoral vigor.

Immediately following Kingson's electoral landslide Team Jesus began setting up and administering the facilities necessary for the Colorado Surgical Jesus Mind Project. Besides stealing vast amounts of money for himself and his cronies, Kingson spent his nearly four years as Pastor Governor mounting an extensive and exhaustive program to surgically alter the human brain toward a more complete Jesus-centeredness. Structural Holiness was to be accomplished by cutting out the evil-inducing parts of the brain and replacing them with Biblically diagrammed bioplastic Jesus-loving bits and parts.

To start, 115,000 sinners were decapitated and their brains carefully scrutinized by the collegium of pataphysicians, mail-order surgeons, debunked and disbarred psychiatric sadists and cranks that headed up the Colorado Surgical Jesus Mind Project for Kingson. The Project protocol targeted 250,000 sinners for various surgical procedures. 178,000 were operated and experimented on, all of whom, eventually, died.

How long would this kind of thing be allowed to go on? Oh, you'd be surprised! The Euros, the Japanese, the PRC and the Soviets did eventually come to a loose agreement on a post-United States world, and finally dispatched retired South African President Mandela to negotiate an end to the Surgical Jesus Mind Project and the departure (loot in hand) of theocratic tyrant Pastor Governor Kingson. Then UNNAA, almost reluctantly, came into Colorado with their half-hearted efforts to try and make it all better. But no one but the starving and displaced were interested in better.

Gladys picks up her satchel and stands closer to Gus.

"Did, they like, have the Devil in here?"

Maude smirks.

"You're the rocket scientist, Gladys. Right? You don't believe in supernatural stuff. Right?"

Gladys presses her lips together and keeps silent.

Gus unbuttons his parka enough to get at his dagger if needed. His small flashlight in hand, he heads inward.

"Let's go in."

"Oh, shit, Gus. It's, like…really…gross, in there…."

Maude shoves Gladys and says:

"Ha-ha. Satan's gonna get your ass bitch. Chop, chop, chop you up for dog food."

Gladys steps away from Maude.

"That's what Satan likes. Doggie, doggie, doggie…."

Gus gives Maude a look. Maude laughs, grabs Gladys and holds her close as the three of them pick their way through the dark entry hall. Gus' narrow flashlight beam just barely reveals a safe path forward.

Most of the building that they explore is dark and stinks. In one side wing there is a short row of narrow confinement cells still in fair shape. One cell has its small window, way up high, broken out. It's cold, but the fresh air helps cut the lurking stink. The cell is dry and feels private.

Gus clears the cell of rubbish and then he drags in a couple narrow nearly undamaged mattresses from a nearby hall. They are the foundations for this night's nest.

Maude drops her satchel and gets out some candles. Gladys shrugs and says:

"Can I…eat some of the bread?"

Maude shrugs, but Gus says:

"No, save it for morning. Have the fruit cocktail stuff UNICEF gave out today."

"It's not enough. I'm, like, really hungry…still."

Gus and Maude are getting their bedding out and set up. Gus gestures toward his satchel where the canned fruit is and he says:

"You can have Maude's too."

Maude nods and adds:

"And you still got yours, Glad. Right?"

Gladys nods.

"See. You'll be full, and ready to sleep."

Gladys sits on her haunches and eats from a small blue container of sweetened fruit.

"Where's yours Maude?"

"Just a second."

"Gus? Gus, when you go pee, you gotta take me with you."

"I can piss without your help."

"Gus…. It's, like, too dark…out there…for me…."

Maude laughs at Gladys.

"You're fucking afraid of Satan. Ain't you?"

Gladys glares. Maude pokes Gus and says:

"Give me a cig."

Gus fishes for a cigarette part.

"Me too, Gus."

"I don't have that many."

Gladys pouts. Gus hands Maude a half cigarette.

"Hurry up, Glad. I'm only doin' bathroom escort once."

"We can't, like, leave the stuff alone."

"There's no one gonna come through that little window. We're just gonna be right in the hall."

Maude shakes her head.

"Huh-uh. Far enough down the hall that I won't smell it all night…."

Jackie Gleason and His Orchestra

"That is so bogus, Gus. Asanowaka could never bring Terao down with some sort of leg or thigh gripping throw.... Terao's legs are just too fat too grip. And anyway, Asanowaka is so tall, a move like that would put him at the disadvantage...."

"What the fuck do you know about sumo throws?"

"As much as you do!"

"I had *two* chances to get into one of the big Los Angeles beyas."

"Oh shit. In your dreams, o-sumo-san."

Gus stands up, takes his zip-up sweatshirt, puts it to his waist, ties the two sleeves behind his back so the sweatshirt hangs in front of him as his maawashi. First Gus stamps each foot as hard as he can. Left, right, left, right. Then he swings both arms out and up so the hands clap together above his head. And he follows through by swinging his right arm back down and curling it so his elbow is extended and his right hand touches his waist. His left arm swings out so that the hand points straight out.

Gladys laughs.

"You're the little teapot...short and stout."

"Fuck you. That was dohyo-iri."

"Very nice ring-entering ritual, o-sumo-san."

"Yeah, that was cool, Gus. But, you're getting too skinny now."

Gus pokes what is now more sagging skin than bulk.

"My stomach is all fucked up."

"Come on, Gus. Get back in bed. I'm cold."

A few minutes later they are all three tucked into their ad hoc nest. Candles are extinguished. For a few moments it is dark and quiet. But then Gus and Maude start groping one another and pulling open each other's clothing. Gladys sits bolt upright and yells:

"Goddamnit! The one night we get, like, someplace quiet…like, a chance for real sleeping…and you two gotta…do that!"

Maude stops kissing Gus, turns to Gladys, smiles and asks:

"Do what?"

Gus shimmies down his heavy canvas trousers and long john underwear. Frustrated Gladys yells:

"Some of these are my blankets!"

Maude and Gus turn their heads and glare.

Maude leans out from under Gus and points out to the dark hall.

"Take your fucking blankets! Right? Go find your own room. Right?"

Gladys stands there shaking angrily. Gus sits up and pokes Maude.

"That's real helpful, Maude."

Gus turns to Gladys.

"C'mon, Glad. Get back in bed. We got a nice warm nest."

Gladys is silent, arms crossed.

Gus pulls up his trousers.

"Here, Glad. Look. We'll make you a little nest all your own. But near us…. See?"

Gus makes a nest for Gladys out of most of the blanketing.

35

"See? Plenty of room. But we're right here."

"Now you can sleep all the fuck you want. Right?"

Gus pokes Maude again, then he gives Gladys a piece of chocolate he'd ferreted away in one of his two satchels.

"Alright? C'mon, Glad."

Maude reaches up and pushes Gladys down into the blanket nest that is a meter or so from her and Gus. Gladys sits, arms crossed. Gus grimaces and looks at Maude.

"Whatever."

Maude lies down. Gus fishes in his satchel.

"Alright, Gladys. Look, this is it. Here, I got four batteries...."

Gus doesn't even have to finish this sentence before Gladys dives for her own satchel and the Ultra PlayDeck 8220 inside.

Gladys takes the rubber band–bundled batteries.

"New?"

"I was standing there when he opened the sealed pack."

Gladys loads the batteries into her gaming deck. She gives Gus and Maude a look.

"You shoulda, like, just given 'em to me. That was stupid."

"Great. Now leave us alone. Right?"

Gus and Maude start to settle back down into each other's arms.

"You had some of that blunt left...."

Gus stops and frowns.

"That little bit of skunk weed...isn't gonna do anything...."

Now Maude pokes Gus.

"Give it to her."

"Fuck."

He digs in one of his two satchels and produces a small folded piece of torn brown paper bag. Gladys smiles and

36

grabs the small brown paper square. Inside the folds is the burnt and resiny butt of a cigar-sized joint made of free-range marijuana off the roadside sprinkled with a little of the good bud smuggled in by the Western troops.

Gladys is very happy gripping the little treasure packet. Considering how shitty it all looked a few minutes ago.

Gladys puts the head phones on and then unwraps the roach. She moves one of the slow-burning candles, anchored on a small piece of rubble, closer to her bed. Gladys sticks her tongue out at Maude and Gus. But they are already going at it again. She holds the roach near the flame until the cherry smolders, and then she takes a small toke, exhales, smiles and pulls aside one headphone and loudly says:

"And don't, like, throw your gooey jimmies where I'm gonna…you know…step on them…."

Gladys laughs, replaces her head phones, and touches the roach to the small candle flame. A couple more short puffs and then Gladys carefully extinguishes the now even resinier and blacker roach bit and folds it back into the brown paper.

Gladys gets down inside the blankets and turns facing away from the couple fucking.

When she powers up the electronic machine, it beeps, and the tone warms Gladys' heart.

Perry Como

In the morning the inquisitorial hospital is dripping damp cold rain and the kids make a little fire and boil some coffee grounds. They add a couple amphetamine tablets. The brew has the right perkiness effect, but doesn't taste much like coffee. They eat the remaining bread so that the sort-of-coffee doesn't give them indigestion.

Gladys, Gus and Maude pack up and explore a couple sections of this former Surgical Jesus Mind Center.

Most of this Center was burned to the ground in the bloody strife of the few months between when Kingson went into exile and the UN occupation of Colorado.

Once he was convinced that UNNAA would use force to shut down the Surgical Jesus Mind Project, all Kingson really wanted was a guaranteed exit. Pastor Bill's family and essential Team Jesus superdooperplenipotentiaries left Colorado aboard Kingson's jetliner, *Team 1*. *Team 1* was followed heavenward by six other Jumbos bearing several tons of pilfered, extorted and stolen wealth all turned into gold and silver bullion.

The seven Jumbos, emblazoned with the bloody Team Jesus crucifix, ascended at sunset out of Denver International in an upward arcing chain. Bound for the sunny beaches of some unspecified equatorial off-shore nation.

The three kids sit on a teetering heap of toppled steel file cabinets. They share a cigarette bit.

"No, before we go wait for a train, I want Gus to tell a story."

"We've heard all his stories.... Right?"

"C'mon, please?!..."

Gladys looks at the older kids. Gus shrugs noncommittally.

"Tell us about presents he bought you...."

"I want to get to the train...."

"C'mon...."

"Yeah, OK.... But, give me a cig."

"I don't have any...."

Gus holds his open palm toward Gladys. Gladys frowns.

"I've only got, like, two...little butts...."

"Fuck you, then. Let's get going...."

"All right. Shit. Here."

Gladys digs around in her satchel and finds the two partly smoked cigarettes and gives them to Gus. He leans back.

Sergio Mendes and Brasil '66

Simple perspective. Calvin Rodriguez, late-40s, chunky, middle-class hispanic man fucking Gus. Gus is younger in this scene by half-a-dozen years. Early teens. (Or just less obvious wear and tear?) Even at this age Gus is 14 or 15 centimeters taller than Calvin.

They are in the livingroom. Neo-Mediterranean stylings and decor. The livingroom is dimly lit. One lone large table lamp—the base a meter and a half tall pottery conquistador (this lamp's twin, at the other end of the sectional sofa, is an aztec warrior) and the shade a map of the "New World"—is turned on to the second of three settings. Large factory knock-off Oriental carpet fills much of the room. Burnished-metal-appearing plastic sconces and pseudo-conquistadorial wall hangings. Blackened wrought-iron candelabras and treatments and fixtures. Sectional sofa and matching easy chairs and accompanying large footstools, all heavy dark wood and overstuffed lush red velvet fabric.

Big, circa-1971 console radio/hi-fi/TV combo unit fills the center of one wall of the livingroom. Dark wood, steel and vacuum tubes. Heavier than death. The radio is on. 1950s through 1970s Pop orchestral tunes, some with sappy choral accompaniment. Just what Calvin likes. The current song is a big moody string and choral piece by Ferrante and Teicher.

Gus' hands and knees are braced on the dark burnt-orange shag carpeting, Gus holds the right position.

Gus listens to the song and to Calvin's pitch and pace.

When Gus is here is this room getting fucked he likes to look out the big picture window that overlooks the big backyard.

This picture window is to the right of a sliding glass door that opens to the big wood deck and wood steps down to the backyard.

Large, downward-sloping sweep of green lawn. Half-acre lot. Many tall pine trees. Out back between the concrete patio and the garden shed, there is a sodium lamp high on a pole.

There have been spring and summer nights, with Gus in this same circumstance, when the sodium yard light out there was a swarming solar system of careening insect orbits. Tonight it is raining. A steady cold pouring rain.

Sonic snapshot: Rain drumming, drenching the wood deck and roof. Underneath that is the song on the radio. And up top of it all Calvin's spiraling urgent fucking efforts.

Calvin's grip tightens at Gus' pudgy waist. Soon is time. Soon. Calvin tensing pressing.

"Say...it...now...."

Gus is daydreaming through the big picture window. He turns his head a bit. Calvin repeats his plea.

"Say...it...."

Gus looks at the picture window. In the reflection he can see Calvin and the livingroom. Beyond that reflection the rain-blurred blob of the sodium light. Gus says the magic word.

"Daaaddy.... Daddy...."

Calvin's tight broken gasping noises erupt in response. Repeat the word. Repeat it, repeat it. Plaintive boy voice. Gus knows the way. Calvin heaving.

41

In the window reflection Gus watches Calvin. When Calvin's noises fade and his pace falters, Gus relaxes and slumps forward a little, still on hands and knees. Sweaty and soggy, Calvin rubs his face on Gus' back.

Gus looks over at the array of framed Rodriguez family photos.

The Missus, Ramona Rodriguez. Davy, the teenage son. Barbara, three years younger than Davy. Tina, the youngest. All gone to abuela and abuelo's for five days.

A few murmured *Daddys* as Calvin comes down. All is well. It's Davy's tone and tremble that Gus is helping Calvin have.

Cold wind shakes at the fir trees in the backyard and the trees throughout this subdivision. It is a cold rainy night anywhere you are. Outside in the cold rain, or inside and warm on your hands and knees. The song on the radio is nearly over. The song ends. The radio announcer comes on. A quiet deep male voice. Friendly. Gus stretches some and the announcer says:

"And that last one was Ferrante and Teicher doing the theme to *Midnight Cowboy*...."

Gus likes that. Midnight. Cowboy. Vaquero. He looks back over his shoulder at Calvin, who has collapsed forward from his hard ride. Gus is the horse, or pack mule.

The Rodriguezes have an old black and white photo of a great-grandfather who was a vaquero in northern Mexico. Gus has studied all of their family photos at length. The photo he thinks about most is a photo of that paternal great-grandfather on a horse, near some cows, with two other vaqueros in the background.

Calvin kisses the back of Gus' neck and on down Gus' spine. Gus closes his eyes. Tomorrow, or the next day, Calvin will

42

take him shopping at the mall. New boots, socks and underwear. At least. Gus looks over at the largest of the photos of Davy on the side table.

Gus studies Davy's haircut in the most current photo of him.

Calvin will buy him lots of stuff if Gus gets that haircut.

Gus does not look anything like Davy. But with the haircut, and Gus' magic word at the proper time...everything is possible.

Calvin finally pulls out. Gus slowly eases himself to the carpet. Give his knees a rest. One knee is rug burned a bit.

The Les Baxter
Orchestra and Chorus

Gus sits back. Gladys and Maude look at him. Gus fishes a half a cigarette from a coat pocket, Maude leans forward and lights it with a stick match she strikes on her belt buckle.

Gladys looks at Gus, then Maude, then Gus again. When it is obvious that Gus has no more to say. Gladys can't help herself.

"So, like, what did he *buy* you?"

"What did the haircut looked like?"

Gus puffs on the cig and shrugs. Gladys frowns angrily.

"Jesus, I *hate* when you do that. You always do that shit, Gus. Tell these long stories that fucking go on and on about what the house looked like and about the…sex stuff….And you *never* tell what Rodriguez *bought* you…."

Maude laughs and pushes at Gladys.

They all three stand up. They've gotten cold and stiff and are losing their coffee buzz. Gus says:

"Glad, you're probably gonna wanna take a walk. Right?"

Gus and Maude want to have sex again in the nice cell room. With the mattress and privacy. Gladys is very angry.

"This is so…fucking rude."

Gladys stands there waiting for the older kids to acknowledge that she is not happy. They ignore her. Gus unfastens the gray sleeping bag. Gladys stomps her feet and waves her fists.

44

"Oh, c'mon, you guys...."

Gladys shoves her booted foot at Gus' side.

"Like, we gotta get to the Rodriguezes'...."

The other two shed their outer garments. There is no stopping them. Maude says to Gladys.

"You don't have to go anywhere. Just be quiet. Right?"

"Fuck you...."

"Only for a half-hour, or so...."

"A halfhour! Jesuschrist.... You guys...."

They do this all the time to her. All the time. Gladys is shaking she is so angry.

I'll sneak back while they're doing it and stab them. Cut off Gus' dick.

Gladys throws down her satchel, and pulls out a smaller shoulder bag of essentials. She flips them off and loudly kicks aside rubbish as she leaves the room.

Gladys heads down a corridor dodging wreckage and stinky smells.

At the far end of that corridor Gladys looks back in the direction of the cell Gus and Maude are in.

"Stupid fucking assholes."

At the next intersection, to her left and right the intersecting hall has collapsed. Gladys scrutinizes up ahead to see if it's worth going further.

The corridor looks mostly intact for a long way. Some gaps in the ceiling where the drizzle is coming in. Such as the one coming up. Gladys watches the light rain fall through the gaping hole and splash into a very large puddle.

Then, suddenly, the very next moment, way way on down the long corridor, Gladys sees lights come on. She quickly crouches down against a wall. Rows of fluorescent tubes along the ceiling. Way way on down there.

Gladys can make out people coming and going in the

lit area. After a minute or so the people disappear and the lights go out. Gladys hears distant sounds of a heavy door being shut. A big heavy metal door.

Gladys looks back in the direction of where Gus and Maude are. She glances at the digital face of her little taped-together plastic clock. It hasn't been anywhere near a half-an-hour yet.

Gladys wonders if there are still brain experiments going on down there. But she is more intrigued than scared. The young white girl slowly heads down the hall, staying near the wall, trying to keep her boots out of the deeper puddles.

Empty window frames filled with brambles and bushes.

With some effort and three sections of the lightweight polycarbon wall paneling Gladys bridges the bigger puddles. She comes to the intersecting hallway she'd seen the fluorescent lights on in. The corridor is now lit only by cloudy sunlight through the holes in a nearby wall.

Trying to avoid the naturally higher adult-sized line of sight Gladys crouches and looks around the corner at floor level. Gladys sees a big heavy security door. She looks for cameras but sees nothing obvious. Gladys looks up at the rows of fluorescent fixtures on the ceiling. All in perfect condition. Clean even.

Gladys gets out her little spy-glass thing that Maude found in the purse of a woman they robbed on a train. Gladys studies the security door's small recessed control panel, its alphanumeric pad and various keycard slots.

Looks fully functional. Gladys has got a couple cracker inserts for standard stuff like telecoms and ATMs. But nothing that could touch the door's set up.

Back behind her Gladys hears distant human voices calling out. Gus and Maude.

46

Gladys backtracks dragging the plastic puddle-crossing panels.

Gus and Maude are done and they've brought Gladys' stuff. Gladys is almost too excited to tell them what she found. She keeps shifting from a whisper to a loud staccato.

Maude grabs the younger girl and says:

"Are you sayin'..."

Maude points down the hall.

"...there's people?"

Excited rapid nodding.

"I saw them. Like I said. There's a door...."

"You open it?"

Gladys shakes her head no and answers:

"It's a big security door."

She points at the nearby battered metal frame and twisted metal hinges of what had been a security door.

"Except, like, the one back there works...."

Gus looks ahead in the corridor. Maude walks to one of the broken-out window frames and sticks her head outside and scans the structures far across the way.

"It's one of those...over there...."

Gus follows her pointing fingers and ponders. Maude frowns.

"What? Are we gonna go hang out with them...or something?!"

"We won't get caught.... I just want to see...you know....Why are they still here?"

Maude scoffs:

"No doubt some horrible mind-fuck shit. And I do not want to get anywhere near them. Right?"

Cold wet rainy day. Gus' breath comes out of his mouth and nostrils in gushes of condensed moisture. He scans the near horizon at treetop level. After a minute Gus points to

47

the far side of one wing and up at wisps of steam generated by hot air vented out a camouflaged plastic chimney. All three stare at the quickly disappearing drifts of steam.

The three youths exit the ruined facility and double back and cautiously work their way along the tree line toward the suspect hospital wing. Gus and Maude have their 23 centimeter double-edged daggers inhand.

The scariest is when they cross in the open between the woods and the suspect building.

The kids easily find the tree with the drab-colored, heavy-gauge polycarbon duct running from the wall of the hospital complex out and up the trunk of the tree. Maude remains crouching back from the building in some of the higher grasses. Gus and Gladys are standing between her and the building and treed chimney. The original outer windows are covered with heavy sheets of brick-faced polycarbon. From some of the windows, where the facing doesn't quite meet, light leaks through. Gus cautiously touches the polycarbon conduit. It is warm to the touch and vibrates slightly to the tempo of the ventilation system inside the building.

Gus tries to climb a tree that will let him look down behind a wall. But he is too big. Maude won't even try to help him. She sits in her grassy blind and says:

"This is stupid, Gus."

"You could at least come help boost me up."

Maude snorts derisively and remains sitting.

Maude lost most of her two left middle fingers about a year ago; an elderly man walking a few meters in front of her stepped on a landmine. A steady firm grip with that hand is difficult. But she could help boost him.

Gus turns and looks at Gladys and looks at the tree and

48

then her again. Gladys had already figured it would come around to this. She looks up the tree at where Gus wants her to go.

"Sure, I *could*...."

She looks at Gus.

"I ain't climbing until I get to eat."

Gus steps back, glares at her, and points up the tree.

"You go up there, and use your little telescope to see what's over the wall...and you do a good job...then I'll see what food I got left."

Gladys laughs at Gus.

"You don't got any food left...."

Gus looks at Maude. Maude's fists are clenched at her side.

"I saved it! Right?! I didn't eat all of mine last night. Right?!"

"C'mon, Maude."

"I always give up food to feed you two."

"Fuck you."

"No...fuck *you*.... I don't even want her to go up there."

Despite the arguing Gladys is sure she's going to eat. She greedily prompts:

"If I am going up that tree...."

Maude hefts her own satchel and heads back the way they'd come.

"I'm going on to the MetroWeb station...."

Gus frowns and grabs his stuff and heads after Maude. Suddenly, Gladys is not getting any food, and they're moving again.

Gladys grabs her satchel and runs after them. They all walk in silence. Gladys runs ahead a couple meters and turns and says:

"At least I don't have to climb the fucking tree."

"Yeah, great…. You win, Gladys. What did you win? Huh?"

Evening comes on. The sunset bleeds deep red through the filters of war smoke and ash. The three kids stumble onto an A-line MetroWeb station that is still up and running. As the kids approach the station's entrance Gladys eyes an older caucasian man with a battered metal shopping cart on small wheels. The shopping cart is full of the man's possessions. Nothing about the man or his stuff look worth stealing.

The old man takes a black plastic–wrapped square from the shopping cart. The black plastic–wrapped object is somewhat heavy for his frail build and somewhat slippery in his grip. He manages to set the package down on the cement alongside the station wall.

The three kids enter the station and the guy pushes his cart on, leaving the package and station behind.

The usable entrances to this MetroWeb station are controlled by a couple detachments of local gangsters turned militia (mostly whites). They inflict an entry fee on all. The kids give up too many things to get in.

The station is already crowded. Outside more and more people are trying to buy their way in. Gus surges forward.

"C'mon, let's move up front."

It takes nearly a half-hour of Gus leading and pushing to get them within three or four meters of the platform edge. Gladys pulls her coat closed and complains:

"Like, why'd we have to come so fucking far out? It's cold."

"Yeah. Let's move back, so we're more under the roof…."

Maude points to where a large square metal garbage bin is home to a roaring fire. People are standing around the fiery barrel, as close as they can afford to pay for. The three kids can afford not-too-close, but close enough so that the general surrounding body warmth is good. Maude is starting to take off her satchel when the package the old man left out near the station's entrance explodes. It is a powerful bomb.

The explosion punches in the outer wall of the building. The rest of the station collapses with it, inward, toward the tracks.

It is the shock wave of the collapsing station, not the bomb blast itself, that throws the kids, and the rest of the people around the barrel of fire, onto the train tracks.

The hot barrel, and the fire it contains, are tossed and spilled onto the tracks and falling refugees. Gladys is stuck under a dead man, Gus drags her out. The three companions scramble and scuttle across the tracks, fleeing the panic and destruction.

Herb Alpert and the Tijuana Brass

Two extra days are used detouring a cluster of neo-traditional fortified hamlets built by Pastor Governor Kingson for his Team Jesus bureaucrats and their codependents. Several hundred residential sextiplexes, half-a-dozen sub-mini strip malls behind double rows of six-meter-high electrified fence.

Happy holding tanks for the techno-managerial strata integral to any End Time state.

With the proximity of functional consumer society the kids are able to find a working payphone. Gladys uses her jacked phonecard so Gus can make one of his calls to the Rodriguezes' voicemail. Gladys smirks:

"Just 'cause they're paid up on voicemail doesn't mean the Rodriguezes are still living in that house you talk about."

Gus frowns at Maude. Maude is exasperated and she tauntingly adds:

"Why don't you leave Calvin a message? Let him know you wanna come home. Right? He can wire us money. I'm tired of stealing…."

Gus ignores her and walks to the payphone.

When they finally arrive at a functional MetroWeb station it is late afternoon and getting cold. Cloudy and cold enough to snow in town. It's been snowing off and on already in the upper elevations. The Rockies are white tombstones along the sundown horizon.

Gus adapts a sumo frontal thrust-out maneuver to push through the milling crowd toward the tracks. Gus is still a big bulky guy, but now his constantly upset stomach, and the new civil wars, are eating at his once-sizable mass.

Once they're in a good spot the kids un-shoulder their satchels. Maude and Gladys pass their time sorting stolen IDs and carefully and delicately supplementing their own documents. Maude gestures derisively at Gladys' European Union ID.

"They give that EU shit out to anyone. Right?..."

Gladys flinches her nostrils and shrugs. Maude scoffs.

"You just like the colors...."

"So?..."

Maude shrugs and shakes her head negatively.

The three youths love to talk exit visas and transit sponsorships. Maude and Gladys are very big on Bulgaria. Gus is nothing but derisive about the Soviet Bloc.

"The only reason the fucking Soviets are left is 'cause the Commies go sooo slooow."

Maude sneers. Gus sneers back and adds:

"Besides...you heard that soldier...the Soviets don't want anyone but scientists...."

Maude ignores this immovable mountain her partner always throws at her. She goes back to her attack.

"The United States dried up. GNR...or one of them megabig companies...got nervous and moved the money out...off-island, or whatever....And the United States dried up. Right?"

Now Gus scoffs.

"GNR? That's just bullshit. Everyone knows there's no fucking company called GNR. That shit's just...an excuse."

"Fuck you, dickhead. They may not be called

53

GNR…but one of them big businesses out there…*they* got the money."

Gus frowns. Maude presses.

"And when they're good and fucking ready GNR will come back in, with the money, and get everything set back up. Right?"

Gus is outraged.

"America went fast and burned out. We were always the fastest!"

This familiar line of bickering stops with the rumbling approach of a train. This one is on the through tracks. It is a full-size freight train, not meant for these commuter tracks. It moves slow and steady, the commuter tracks sagging.

It is not a troop train, it is not a transport train.

Special train. A big Team Jesus white crucifix crudely swathed across the side. Another sure sign that the UNNAA ceasefire has collapsed under the weight of God and money.

Special trains transporting un-americans and de-americans to a simple destination. No more Surgical Jesus Mind Project for Team Jesus to keep supplied with fresh brains, but so what! Ingenuity is the United States' middle name!

Maude turns away. Gladys stares after the disappearing train. This special train makes the young white girl think of a song. She hums a few bars. The train moves out of sight. Without the visual cue of the train Gladys' humming is disjointed, meaningless. She can't remember the rest. No one could. Kingson's theocracy and the civil war that followed his departure watered down social memory so severely that it's a wonder anyone in Colorado even remembers to breathe.

The last thing that any American could really clearly remember was the sale of the U.S. Midwest to pay-off some of the back interest due on the nation's debt. All the land from the Canadian border to Texas was transformed into the world's largest pork factory farm. Heartland Hog Holdings.

Which the corporate owners claimed could easily keep the peoples of the earth in pork for the next 6,000 years.

The actual factory farm complex itself only covers the northern half of the territory; the southern million square kilometers is an interlocking series of vast seas of porcine waste.

After that, the staggering steps toward the end of the former United States were all sort of inevitable. Even First Lady-for-Life Nancy Reagan couldn't put the pieces together again. Many, especially the Secret Rapture Movement, said it was all Biblically foretold. Especially the Great Quake. The Great Quake that hit the central East Coast of the former United States instead of the West Coast and finally ended the 30-year run of the Ron and Nancy Show. As well as shedding from the continent much of the Eastern Seaboard. Leaving the Statue of Liberty, battered and worn, tilting at an angle, and buried up to its waist in sand along the new post-quake beachline.

The three kids go back to waiting for a train. Maude is thinking about when she was 11 and pitched a season of shutouts for her Little League team. Gladys is also reminiscing about her own childhood. As he usually does when waiting, Gus works through in his mind throws he'd use to defeat various famous rikishi.

Lawrence Welk and the Champagne Musicmakers

Gus offers halves of cigarettes to the girls. Even after the bloody class and sectarian devolution of the former United States there are still plenty of cigarettes. Maude looks up as she exhales cigarette smoke. Two guys (one white, one mixed-race) are heading toward them. Maude pokes her two companions. The three kids stand and shoulder their satchels. Maude and Gus grip their daggers. Gladys steps behind her older friends.

"Hey, can you spare a cigarette?"

The caucasian stranger tightens his fists, staring at Maude. Both men keep getting slowly closer. Gus flashes his big shiny dagger, the two men stop. Gus throws two cigarettes to the man who spoke.

"Thanks, man. Where you guys headed?"

None of the three kids answer. The caucasian man is getting real close to Maude. Maude whips out her dagger. The stranger leers and reaches inside his own coat for a weapon. Maude leans forward and with a solid strike of her dagger slices deep through the sleeve of the man's coat, undergarments and flesh to the white of his forearm bones. He grunts and grips the bleeding wound. The three youths retreat several paces.

At the other end of the platform a squad of long unpaid police storm into the station wielding their electro-batons. The cops apply their skills in the traditional ways of disgruntled police—brutality and theft.

The crowd panics. Stampeding this way. Stampeding that way.

In the midst of this chaos a damaged train approaches the station. A rickety string of box cars, one or two commuter cars, and several flatbeds that've been converted with sheets of vinyl and aluminum over polycarbon frames into rube goldberg passenger cars. Gus grabs his two friends and they run for the train as it is screeching to a stop. The panicked crowd of refugees also shifts momentum toward the train.

The three kids make it to one of the commuter cars just a few meters ahead of the trampling mob. Gus steps in between the closing doors and heaves with his shoulder and the sliding doors pop back open. Cranky electronic buzz buzz. The crowd surges, nearly engulfing Gladys. Maude slashes at them with her dagger. Gladys jumps into the train car.

The conductor of this section of the train is sticking his head out a window, firing a compact-frame submachinegun and yelling. At Gus? The crowd generally? The gunfire scatters the weak hearted.

The train smashes into a barricade on the tracks and Gus slams forward banging his head against the edge of the sliding door. Gus is seeing stars and not firm on his feet. Maude tries to get on, but Gus sags and starts tilting out the door. Maude shoves at her partner and she yells:

"Pull on him, Glad!"

Gladys yanks Gus as Maude shoves again. Gus stumbles inside. Maude comes crashing in, still pushing at him. The doors slam shut.

More gunfire. The train accelerates.

Maude jumps to her feet. Gus remains sitting on the train car floor. Gladys stands clutching Maude and a pole near the door. The train rapidly picks up speed.

A man runs up to the closed doors. He pounds on the plastiglass, but this door's panes are solidly in place. The train accelerates relentlessly. The man stumbles with a shriek.

Gladys shakes her head.

"Christ. It's not, like, this is the last train, or whatever."

Ray Stevens

Along the opposite side of the car that the three youths land in are a dozen or so mostly sleeping Golden West Guards (mostly white). The 11-rayed golden sun emblazoned on their arm and chest patches. Low-end, noncom, officers. Low-end maybe, but their submachineguns, their rations, their warm dry uniforms....

One soldier (white), a corporal, is not asleep. He watches the kids' chaotic entry into the car. He sits up.

"Hey you...colored girl."

Maude turns. She smiles and says:

"Yes, sir?"

"Let's see some ID."

He stares from Gladys to Gus and from Gladys to Maude. The corporal points at Gladys.

"She yours?"

Maude shakes her head no. Gus makes himself stand up.

"Cindy's...my little sister."

"Who's she then?"

The finger is on Maude. Gus' blood pressure rises. The biggest veins along his temples pulsate. Maude opens her coat, enough to have access to her dagger, if it comes to that.

Now other of the Guard noncoms are grumbling about being roused from their sleep or stupor. Gus grabs the two girls. One of the awakened officers (mixed-race) yells at the initial inquisitor.

"Give it a fucking rest, Gunderson. I'm trying to fuck-ing sleep before Fort Collins."

Gunderson starts to say something. The other noncom,

a sergeant, cuts him off.

"I'm sleeping, right?!"

"Yes, sir!"

Gus pushes his friends to the forward end of the car.

In the next car up Gus leans against a pole, slides down and rests crouching on his big dirty boots. Maude and Gladys clean and patch his forehead gash. Gus pushes aside their hands. He stands and takes a deep breath.

"I'm alright."

Gus grabs his satchels and motions toward the car ahead.

"C'mon."

Percy Faith and His Orchestra 1.O

No safe robbery prospects on this train. It passes several abandoned and wrecked stations. When it finally stops at a functional station the kids detrain. There they settle down to wait for the next train, and hopefully more fertile petty criminal pastures.

Gus' head aches and he is a little nauseous. Gladys yawns and stretches and says:

"Tell us another story, Gus. About Christmas."

"I was only there one Christmas."

Maude smirks:

"Only once? Shit. You tell *so* many Christmas stories…. Right? I thought you were always going to the Rodriguezes' for holidays…."

"Fuck you."

Gladys scoffs:

"Maude's jealous…."

Maude hits Gladys in the face. Gladys grabs her face and yells:

"Fuck you, asshole!"

Gus says loudly and firmly.

"Come on, knock it off."

Gus looks at Gladys' face.

"You're fine. Shut up, both of you…."

Gus sits back and says:

"I'll tell a Christmas story you haven't heard before."

The Fifth Dimension

Snow for Christmas. Not so uncommon for Christmastime in Denver. But this Christmas Gus is younger. This Christmas is six years ago, the former United States is still staggering along, still managing to keeping the Eternal First Couple, Ron and Nancy, in clean clothes.

It's about 11 p.m., Gus has coins enough for three cups of coffee. With the two free refills per paid cup, as long as he shifts seats each cup, Gus can sit out this late-December night in this 24-hour cafeteria, warm and dry.

Gus looks up from watching creamer dissolve into his coffee. His hands go cold and sweaty. There is a man standing across the cafeteria, facing the other direction. From the back the man's coat is like Calvin Rodriguez's coat. From the back the man's haircut is like the way Calvin gets his cut. Gus sort of stands, then he sits back down. This isn't Friday. They always meet on Friday nights. Maybe Calvin is here to meet some new boy on a new night?

Gus watches as the man slowly turns. It is Calvin. He is looking for someone. Calvin's gaze freezes on Gus. Calvin smiles and casually works his way over.

"Hello, Gus. I was hoping you'd be here."

Gus cannot control the redness rising up his face. Calvin sits down, smiles and offers Gus a cigarette.

"What's going on, Gus?"

Gus stutters just a bit.

"Keeping busy...."

"Good, good...."

Calvin stares at Gus, Gus looks into his plastifoam cup of coffee and whitener.

"Ramona and the kids are off to my in-laws for Christmas...."

Gus manages to nod.

"Yeah, but not me...not this year, this is my year to supervise the holiday crew at work. So, I'm...all alone for Christmas."

"That's...too bad...."

"I hate spending Christmas alone...."

Gus takes a drag on his cigarette. His hand a bit unsteady. Calvin leans forward, his big full American face a bit damp.

"If it won't get in the way of *your* holiday plans, Gus.... You could stay with me?...."

Calvin smiles real big and paternal. Calvin is very firm about the pretense that they are not a homeless teenager and a late-40s middle-class accountant.

"What about it? You and me...for Christmas?"

Gus stands up.

"Sure...."

Gus drops his voice as he slyly says:

"Daddy...."

Percy Faith and His Orchestra 1.1

"Yeah, yeah."

Gladys glares at Gus.

"We've *heard* all that."

"You got somewhere you got to go to? Huh, Gladys?"

Gladys ignores him and says:

"I'm hungry. Let's eat the rest of that stuff the Blue Helmets gave out."

Martin Denny and His Orchestra

Compilation of Percy Faith and His Orchestra's Christmas favorites. Soaring cheerful orchestral arrangements.

It sounds super on Calvin's powerful vacuum-tube hi-fi stereo in this big warm split-level home.

"Look here, Gus."

Calvin holds a small shiny red box. Wrapped in a narrow green ribbon with a bow on top.

"Go on. Open it."

Gus' big nervous hands try to be delicate. Calvin impatiently plucks up the lid.

Gus can see a shiny Christmas-tree ornament nestled in the tissue paper.

Calvin and Gus are standing together in front of the big densely decorated and lighted artificial Christmas tree in the Rodriguezes' livingroom. The room is awash in festive holiday decor. On one wall closely spaced strings of flashing green lights festively spell out "Happy," and on another wall flashing strings of red lights spell out "Holidays." A third wall is covered in Christmas cards. The family's icon of Mary and Child, usually off-limits in the DRESS-UP ROOM, is perched on a nest of shiny blue fabric on the wide slate hearth.

"Get it out. Go on."

Gus ever so carefully takes out the red glass globe.

Silvery glitter painted on the globe in the outlines of angels. A red glitter ribbon painted around the top. On opposing sides of the sphere are two deep indentations with a saint's face painted in each one.

"Every couple years the family adds ornaments to the tree...."

Calvin takes the ornament and removes the metal cap from the glass neck at the top of the globe, revealing Gus' name delicately hand-lettered there around the neck.

Gus is standing with the big plastic Christmas tree behind him. His jeans and his underwear are down around his ankles. His sweaty hands gently coddle his Christmas ornament. Calvin is kneeling in front of Gus. Gus' eyes are closed and his face is a twitching conflict of concentrations as he orgasms in Calvin's mouth.

Percy Faith and His Orchestra 1.2

Maude laughs. Gus grins. Gladys complains:

"Christ, we *knew* that, without you saying it."

"So, you got...a stupid Christmas ornament?"

"Did you take it with you, Gus?"

"No, see.... Every year at Christmas, my ornament gets hung with the other family ornaments...."

Maude shakes her head.

"Shit, you're pathetic, Gus.... I am embarrassed I sleep with you. Right?"

"Fuck you. You don't understand what members of families do for each other...."

Maude angrily shoves Gus.

"Fuck you, *loser.* Before Kingson, before the civil war I had a family...."

Maude steps back and vehemently adds:

"Brothers, a sister...and a fucking dog. Right?"

The older kids glare at each other. Gladys interrupts.

"Hey. Here comes a train."

But the train only slows some as it merges off the damaged through tracks. The detour track passes alongside what had been this station's westbound platform. This train is not stopping here. Several thousand displaced persons in the station on that platform want on this train.

The refugees charge the still-moving train, flinging themselves at it. Most bounce off or get stuck and are dragged to their deaths. Some manage to get on board through broken-out windows, doors and holes in the train walls.

Conductors, their flunkies and hired guns (mostly whites, some blacks and a few hispanics) shoot into the crowd, trying to keep the would-be entrainers at bay.

Without checking to see that Gus and Maude are following, Gladys leaps through a broken train window. Maude tries to follow Gladys, but an older white man is also squirming through the same window. She kicks at him and the man falls away with a choke and Maude tumbles inward, landing near Gladys.

The train is going faster, heading out of the station. Gus grips the window frame and runs along. But the train moves faster than he can run. Gus strains to pull himself inside. The train moves faster. He is hanging from the window. The train is approaching a narrow passage porticoed by concrete pillars. Gus pulls and pulls, his face is red scared. Maude grabs his shoulders and she yanks as Gus heaves and he catapults inside just before the narrow passage.

The cars on this train are too crowded for robbery. The kids work their way forward.

One car has no ceiling at all. In it are fiery grills in open-top steel barrels. Grilling meat and vegetables on thin wood skewers.

The three kids stop. There is a little back-and-forth. Gus pays with a couple unopened packs of Chinese Marlboros and three silver finger rings.

Maude points to a kabob near the back, blackened by the steady nearness of fire.

"Yeah, that one."

Gladys watches the kabob Maude gets.

"I want mine from up front. I like rare."

"Sure, girlie…."

Maude studies the pieces of meat on the stick she's been given and then smells it. One of the vendors evil-eyes her. She ignores him and says:

"Make hers well-done too."

"No. Not mine."

"All three of 'em. Right?"

Gladys scowls.

"Ick."

The kids chew the darkened meat and veggies as they work their way through two trashed and skeletal cars, completely open to the air and sloshing around with rain water and urine and shit.

"I hate meat this burnt."

"It was all filthy. We'll be lucky if even this doesn't give us the shits."

"I like the meat…."

Maude scowls as she picks the veggies off the skewer.

"You're crazy…."

Gladys answers with:

"Then…can I, like…have your meat?"

"You know what kind of shit they cook up? Right? Here doggie doggie…."

Maude waggles her skewer at them. Gladys repeats:

"Do you want your meat?"

Johnny Mercer and His Orchestra

A few more cars on ahead the crowd thins out. Gus and Maude are getting strong smells of victim. The kids move on up one more car. This one is not very full at all. There's a couple lone dataserfs, and these two young women. One caucasian american, the other mixed-race american. Clean clothes and clean skin. With assorted kids, all similarly scrubbed and outfitted.

As Gus, Maude and Gladys pass the trixies and their broods Gladys stares at one little girl's green plasticotton leggings.

Gus pulls up short at the other end of the car. Gladys steps ahead of Maude and tugs at Gus' parka sleeve.

"That girl back there...she had these leggings...."

Gus is busy and he only mutters:

"Huh?..."

"The girl back there...."

Gus is not paying attention as he turns back toward the trixies. Gladys falls in beside Maude, who's securing her satchel on her back so she'll have both hands free.

The three kids move very fast. Suddenly Gus is looming in front of the two women, Gladys is on his one side and Maude the other. Maude uses her ugly anger voice and barks:

"Money!"

The women grab their kids and one of the trixies starts to speak and Maude punches her hard in the face.

"Don't say nothing! Right?! Give us your money!"

The trixies hold out purses. Gus checks the white woman's hand bag. Nearly a hundred Golden West credits and two fresh A-level corporate ration cards. Nothing is scarce with these cards. The mixed-race woman's purse is empty of valuables. Gus yells at the mixed-race woman:

"Dressed like that! You got money."

She hurriedly says:

"Her husband gets all the goodies.... I stick with her."

The injured white woman, jaw dislocated by Maude's powerful right punch, tries to shake her head no, as she looks at Gus fearfully.

Gladys grabs the shoulder of the girl wearing the green leggings.

"I want your tights!"

The girl makes frightened noises and huddles against her mother. Gladys scowls and slugs the girl. The girl hollers.

Gus looks around at the other people in the car. A few Tribbers, but they're too busy praying to care about crime. The dataserfs fled the car as soon as the crime started. Gus is still pumped on anger and he kicks the white woman very hard with his big heavy boot. The woman shrieks through her fucked-up mouth.

Gladys yanks off the girl's loafers and then strips the tights off her. The girl limply weeps, clinging to her battered mother. Maude yanks two rings off one woman's hand, looks at them and tosses them to the floor. Gladys stuffs the tights in a parka pocket. Gus nods and they all three run forward.

Their uptrain passage is stymied by another overwhelmingly packed car. The train groans and steel wheels shriek as the train shifts tracks to pull into an approaching station.

Gus pushes his way to a window, climbs onto a trashed seat frame and sticks his head out the partly broken-out window. He looks back at the end of the train. Several cars back the woman they just robbed is also sticking her head out a broken window. She points at Gus. An asian american train conductor is leaning out of the same window, he stares at Gus. Gus ducks back in.

"As soon as it stops we gotta get out of here."

The train pulls up alongside the platform. Hundreds are waiting to get on this train. Behind them a couple thousand more push to get into the station.

Instead of stopping the train lurches and accelerates.

"Shit."

Gus steps back, braces on a pole and kicks out the rest of that plastiglass window.

"Glad!"

Gladys leaps up next to him and he grabs her by the seat of her jeans and coat collar and steadies her on the rim of the window a second before she leaps out. She lands on several people and then drops to the concrete platform. Gus dives out of the train window next, and Maude quickly follows.

The train is really moving when Maude jumps. As she leaps she looses her balance and crashes down into the crowd. Legs and arms akimbo. Maude's head smacks into the concrete platform. She blacks out for a second. Gus is right there and he tugs her up enough so she isn't trampled in the crowd.

"Maude! Come on...."

Maude pulls herself back into consciousness enough to sit up.

"Yeah....Yeah, OK."

Gus helps her stand. They head into the crowd looking for Gladys.

Gladys is being carried by the tidal wall of humans and is already several meters to their right. Those near the front of the platform are struggling to avoid the edge and the moving train. Those in the back are pushing forward unknowingly.

Gladys stays low and uses her folding knife to keep hands off her. She sees Gus' big head over the other refugees. Gladys jumps straight into the air, so her feet are a meter off the concrete. She yells and waves and as she drops back to earth Gus' head snaps over and he sees Gladys disappearing back down into the crowd.

It takes a minute or two of Gus and Maude fiercely elbowing and ham-fisting through the swirling mob until they get to Gladys, who is now crouched with her back to a metal pillar.

Gladys and Maude grip the back of Gus' parka as he wades on through the thousands more people flooding into the station, all still expecting the train to have stopped.

There are people in some makeshift uniforms. Militia loyal to one or the other would-be Kingson successor. Their main badges of authority are their submachineguns. Gus ignores them. The paramilitaries are mostly interested in keeping the increasingly frustrated and angry crowd from lynching them.

Outside in the nearby parkinglot of a former strip mall the UNHCR has set up big pots of lukewarm vitamin-fortified mush. Gladys, Gus and Maude wait in line. Each gets a full plastic bowl of the vitamin-fortified gruel. The three drink the sweetened and flavored sludge. The bland mush sits well on Gus' stomach and he sighs, contented to feel full and not sick as a result. Gladys offers the rest of hers and he gladly drinks it and then smiles his thanks and says:

"Good stuff."

Mel Torme and His Orchestra

The heavier aspects of the post-Kingson civil war never really reached this far-western side of metro Denver. Intersecting avenues of former strip malls that are still mostly intact and serving as open markets.

The indoor shops and stalls are too expensive for the kids. The parkinglots are full of trade from car trunk, hand cart, pickup truck bed, blanket and tarp spread across the ground.

The three peruse several blocks of traders, recyclers and scavengers. They trade some costume jewelry, two watches, and a couple odds-and-ends ID documents for a new thermal blanket, a new wet stone and two packs of filterless Mexican Delicado cigarettes.

They find a tall caucasian american man who's got a lot of pornography spread out for sale. Gus shows this man a couple of the photos Maude found in a bag the kids stole from an old white couple on a train. They are photos of adults (various races) having sex with children and teenagers (various races). The man has no glasses with his prescription, so he bends close to the photos and studies them a minute or two.

"OK."

The trader walks to his handcart.

"C'mon, over here."

From an anonymous plastic bag the man brings out a metal box. He gestures for them to come closer. He opens the metal box. Nothing much that they want. Maude stands up and starts to get the sample photos back when Gladys' hand dives into the box and pushes aside some stuff and pulls out a small 15mm square electronic component.

"This, Maude."

Maude stares at the tiny electronic component.

"That?"

"It'll really boost my cracker card...."

Maude looks at Gus. Gus always keeps a flat nothing face on when Maude's trading. And he doesn't know any more about electronics than Maude. Maude looks at the small plastic piece and then at Gladys.

"We're not looking for fun and games. Right? Right, Gladys?"

"No. I mean, yes, Maude. No fun and games. You know."

Gladys twitches and tries to restrain herself.

The man looks down at Gladys and then over at Maude. The man reaches in the metal box and pulls out another electronic board, this one even smaller. Gladys' eyes light up. The man smiles gleefully.

"I figure a hot shot like you will want this too."

Maude snaps at the guy:

"Don't encourage her. Right?"

"But these are gonna cost you angels all your family photos...."

The trader waves the samples he's clutching and points to the rest of the snapshots in Gus' hands.

"For all them photos...you get the electronics.... And I'll throw in two credits a piece."

"Four each."

"Two and a quarter,"

Maude snatches the photos out of the man's hands. The trader shrugs.

"OK, OK. Two seventy-five."

Maude replies:

"So you can sell them as souvenirs to the Blue Helmets, for 10 or 15 a piece? Right?"

"Three. Or go away."

By way of acceptance Maude says:

"No UNNAA scrip. Yen or Atlanta Dollars. Right?"

The man laughs.

"Atlanta Dollars. Ah, you're in vaudeville…and kiddie porn, huh, girlie?"

Maude doesn't get it and isn't interested. The trader shrugs trying to look helpless in the face of such demands.

"You think I gotta box of Atlanta Dollars?!"

"Shut the fuck up with that shit."

"I got two hundred New Yen and four hundred Golden West Credits."

"What series?"

"Blue."

Maude checks the money as the white guy forks it over. Especially the Golden West credit squares. Only the blue series are valid anymore, and they're easy to counterfeit.

The kids go to a small coffee stall. The proprietor is a big cranky african american guy in the corner on a folding chair in front of a narrow table with four hot plates set out in a row. On one burner is steadily simmering coffee, the one next to that is rice and beans, third is goulash with meat and the fourth is a type of sweetened grain gruel that people pour high proof alcohol over, let it soak, and then slurp down.

All of which are served up in the same-sized small plastic tubs. Gus orders a bowl of the grain mash, with no booze, and three bowls of coffee. While the man looks at the Golden West credits Gus gave him Gladys asks:

"Why do you get to eat, and not me?"

"This stuff's easy on my stomach. You can eat anything."

Gus gulps the bowl of sweetened grain mush.

There are no chairs in the stall except the proprietor's. The kids stand and slurp at their cups. The stall's proprietor has a small flat-screen TV on the wall to his left. He flips between a prayer marathon and coverage of terrorist trials.

"Excuse me. Excuse me.... Sir. Hey, sir. The Tokyo autumn tournament is on TV4.... Satogayama is up for promotion to ozeki if he does well...."

The man does not acknowledge Maude. Maude bares her teeth.

Gladys rummages in her satchel and extracts part of a cig she'd stowed. Gus snatches it away and she punches his arm. Gus ignores her and lights the smoke. Gladys stares as Gus deeply inhales.

"Christ, Gus. You're...a fucking monster...."

Gus sneers, grabs his crotch and shakes it at her. Gladys smirks. Gus hands Gladys the cig, she starts to step away, Gus reaches out and grabs her. He says:

"Don't go off with the smoke..."

Gladys takes a drag and makes to hand it back. Gus relaxes his grip to reach for the cigarette bit and Gladys jumps away and lands next to Maude, who is laughing. Gladys hands the cigarette to her.

Man behind the counter sees their cups are empty. He shuffles over with the heavy saucepan he ladles the boiled coffee out of.

"Another cup?"

Gus looks from girl to girl, they shake heads no. Gus looks at his cup and then at the man and shrugs.

"No, thanks...."

The man settles back in his perch at the four hot plates, one hand on the TV remote. Without looking again at them he says:

77

"Get out of here."

"Hey, we paid."

The man's right hand, the hand not clutching the TV remote comes up from between his big legs with a 10mm semiautomatic pistol in hand.

The three youths retreat to the street. Now it is raining. Gus gets out his baseball cap and the others follow suit. Above the bill of each kid's baseball cap are the names in kanji characters of a favorite rikishi. Satchels are put on under coats. Keeps their hands free and possessions dry.

It's getting dark. Cold wind brings the rain in waves.

Sammy Davis, Jr.

The kids linger against a wall and watch the street build its nighttime energies. A local posse, marshalling nearby, casts unfriendly glares at the three refugees. So they head down an intersecting street. Street vendors and shops thin out to none and they come up against another fortified hamlet for mid- and low-managers and engineers. All real new. Wind just right, stand just so—that wrapper-just-removed odor is clear and pungent.

It takes Gladys, Gus and Maude the rest of the day to circumvent the walled enclave. They camp in an abandoned dump truck at a never-finished and now-looted building site. The next day they finally get to a major arterial road. That road eventually crosses some MetroWeb tracks. The kids abandon the road to follow the tracks. By then it's nearly nighttime again. They give up looking for a MetroWeb station for the day. Maude spots an unfenced park several blocks away.

The empty park is actually two identical parks separated by an east-west four-lane road. The parks are very new. Lots of tall pruned trees planted in rows and patterns. Carefully landscaped shrubs, flowers and ground coverings. Beauty bark spread out in large decorative swathes. Bordering the southern park is a line of wooded hills. Each park has two gazebos and a bandshell. In the middle of a small cement plaza are flag poles. The flag poles' long metal cords rattle in the wind. A couple of drinking fountains and tiled public restrooms nearby.

About four meters from these public amenities is another public amenity. Courtesy of the former Pastor Governor.

Square concrete slab, 2 x 2 meters. Set in the middle is a heavy steel and plastic pillory. The public flogging harness amenity. The cement inclines to a grated drain opening. Near the harness is a faucet and hose for ease of cleaning. Electrical outlets nearby provide easy setup for local media coverage.

The kids hurry through the park to the wooded hills, they cross near the park's amenities. Gus is very unhappy about going anywhere near the pillory. Maude is gripping him around the waist and pressing him on.

"Don't keep looking at it, Gus. Right? Let's get to the hills."

Gladys is looking at the covered picnicking pavilions as she says:

"It's gonna rain some. You know it is."

Gus scowls and answers:

"We're not sleeping in the park…."

"But, like, I don't wanna sleep in the rain…."

Gus glances back at the pillory.

"No."

Gladys starts to complain more, Maude cuts her off.

"Forget it, Glad. We can, like, find some trees to sleep under…. Right?"

Gus stops at the crest of one of the hillocks and he squats down.

"See. Like, over there. Or, even here…We'll be dry…."

Gladys looks around and shrugs.

"Yeah, OK."

The rain has pretty much stopped. Maude starts to take her satchel off, but Gus stands up and says:

"Naw, I'm not tired yet.... Let's go back to the shops...and get some marijuana."

Gladys does a little dance.

"Yeah! Let's get stoned!"

Gus looks at Maude and she shrugs and says:

"Sure."

Glen Campbell

Halfway back to the parkinglot marketplace to barter for marijuana the rain comes down again, harder and harder, accompanied by thunder and lightening. The youths are passing a back entrance of a wrecked multi-story office building. The plastimetal overhang above the back doorway is still in place. The three kids leap the two cement steps up to a narrow landing in front of the door and huddle. Rain drums steadily on the overhang.

A few moments pass and then cutting through the storm, an anonymous shriek. Then there are other, louder, definitely male shouts. Gladys, Gus, Maude, all three jump, startled, and press against the battered metal door. Gladys slides in behind Gus. Gus has his coat open to access his dagger. Maude is already clutching the hilt of hers.

Around the street corner comes a young caucasian boy, running in a blind panic. About Gladys' build and age, with a Red Cross buzz cut. A few rain-soaked tatters of girl clothing cling to the running shoeless boy.

He is running, faltering, at the end of his strength. He doesn't register Gus, Maude and Gladys. The boy stumbles.

Gus hesitates, then grabs the running boy, lifts him off his feet, and shoves the boy in back under his parka against the wall. With the other hand he pulls Gladys so she stands between and behind him and Maude. Gus straightens up, pokes his hands into his coat pockets, and backs up some so it looks like Gus is standing with his back to the battered metal door.

A hooting barking pack of mallrats (five boys, one girl,

three white, a black, a hispanic and one mixed-race) come thundering around the corner.

The posse careens to a standstill right in front of Gladys, Gus and Maude. They hop and strain to hold still, stoked on adrenaline and amphetamines.

Maude and Gus draw their long daggers. The mallrats' hands grip and flex and tear at the air. These marauder's weapons are more deadly than Gus and Maude's blades, but the posse doesn't want just any trouble.

"The faggot! The little faggot!"

Gus grumbles:

"Some kid…went…down there…."

Gus sort of points in the direction the pack was headed. A tall mixed-race american mallrat yells:

"I get this one first!"

"Fuck you. Let's see who catches him!…"

The shaved-headed hispanic girl and Maude are staring each other down. Girl considers attacking Maude for Maude's dagger. One of the guys yells,

"Let's go!"

"Don't wanna lose that one…."

"Gonna *squeal* that little fuck!…"

They leap and dash down the street. In a moment they are far enough away you can't hear them over the rain and thunder.

Gus, Maude and Gladys stand a moment longer. Gus lifts his coat open and looks back at the crouching trembling boy. He is holding himself tightly. Shivering violently. The boy tries to speak but he is shaking too hard. Gus looks up and down the block. He turns his back to the street and holds his coat open and up, so the kid is out of the rain and view.

"Dry him off with something."

Maude uses some of her dirty clothes to wipe water off

83

the boy. Maude looks at the boy, the boy's torn girl clothes. Gladys twists her satchel around front and opens it.

"He can wear my sneakers."

"I think I got a T-shirt he can wear...."

The boy eyes the clothes inside Gladys' satchel. Without so much as a howdy-do he jerks out of Maude's grasp and grabs a pair of yellow heavy cotton tights out of Gladys' satchel.

"Hey! Those are mine."

The boy tears off his tattered skirt and underwear and then rolls Gladys' tights up his legs. Gladys yells, even angrier:

"They're girls'...."

Gus grumbles.

"Hurry the fuck up."

The boy yanks off the tatters of his old pullover. Maude hands him some dirty clothes. He rubs his torso a bit drier.

The boy looks at Gus, Maude and Gladys. Gus mostly watches the street.

"My name's Walter."

No one gives theirs in return.

Walter puts on Gladys' ratty, knee-length red wool skirt, the blue T-shirt Maude hands him, Gladys' longish bright floral-patterned sweater and then a gray tarp poncho.

Now Gus looks at the boy, dressed in Maude and Gladys' clothes. Gus looks at Maude and she shrugs and he shrugs and he says:

"C'mon."

Gladys complains:

"It's still raining."

"Shut the fuck up."

Gus takes off into the rain.

Walter runs along beside Gladys. She looks at him a couple times before she says:

"You're, like, a boy. And…you got, like, *my* clothes on."

Walter looks at Gladys, shrugs and says:

"I'm, like…your sister."

Walter tries to smile. Gladys frowns:

"You're not like any of my sisters…."

Walter scowls. The rain pours down steadily. Walter's head is drenched and he keeps wiping the water off his face. Gladys pulls out a ratty blue baseball cap with her second favorite sumotori's tegata on the brim. Walter scowls before he pulls the cap snug on his head.

"Hamanoshima? Shit."

"Hey. That's, like, totally fucking fine. Give it back."

Walter hurriedly smiles.

"Sorry, Hama's cool…."

Walter looks up ahead at Gus, who hasn't slowed his long strides and is getting quite a ways ahead of them. Gladys finally smiles at Walter. She says:

"I'm Gladys. That's Gus. That's Maude. They're, like, a couple…."

Walter and Gladys share a restrained grimace.

"We're gonna go sleep in a park…. You wanna come with us?"

Gus stops and unfastens his smaller satchel and hands it to Walter.

"Carry this for me. Don't fuckin' lose it."

Maude looks at Walter shouldering Gus' satchel. Maude asks her boyfriend:

"So, we're…gonna keep him?"

Gus glances at Walter and then smiles.

"I dunno."

Maude frowns at her partner.

"You're the one who grabbed him. Right?…"

Gus gives Maude a sly look.

"Like, when I grabbed him, I thought he was, you

85

know, a bitch."

Maude frowns. Gus smiles and adds:

"Cute maybe…."

Maude turns and hits Gus in the arm. Hard.

Gus runs off ahead. Once he's a couple meters ahead of his partner he turns and looks at Maude and starts chanting loudly.

"New twat, new twat. I…got…some…new twat!…"

"A better fit for your tiny fucking dick. Right? Right, fuckhead?!"

Gus ignores Maude. She picks up a bit of rubble, and hefts it like she's about to pitch a baseball. Gus starts sing-songing again.

"New twat, new twat. I got some new twat…"

A short wind-up and Maude pitches a direct hit at Gus' left calf and he stumbles and drops and catches himself as he nearly twists his leg.

"Ouch!! Fuck you, bitch."

"Fuck you, dickface."

The now four kids make their way back to the hills that are along the southern edge of the southern park. Up in the hills they follow the trodden paths around flare-ups of brush and brambles.

Gus is on point. Maude sniffs and scrunches her face.

"Smell that?"

Gus stops and holds out his hand to stop the others. They ignore him and hurry forward.

What was once a human is now a desiccated carcass. Discernible as human only by its framing of bones and scraps of clothing that still cling. Grass and blackberry vines have pushed up through the remnants.

"Eeew."

"Gross."

Maude pushes at it with a boot toe. They all watch. Gladys says:

"It's still a person. "

Walter retorts:

"Bones are not, like, a person."

"Bones are a person. That's their, you know, skeleton."

"Are bones a person, Gus?"

"Get the fuck away from it. Never touch a rotted body. They got all sort of germs and shit."

Maude sees some sort of a satchel under the skeletal remains and clothing. She gets out her dagger and fishes the satchel from the bones.

"Give it a rest, Maude. It's, you know...grave robbing."

Gus steps away and frowns at his partner.

"Once they're that dead, Maude, you gotta leave 'em alone."

The scavenged satchel was long ago cut wide open and emptied, probably back when whoever they were was killed. Gus kicks dirt and leaves at Maude.

"C'mon...."

Walter and Gladys have moved on ahead, holding hands and staying very close to each other, carefully scanning where they are about to step.

It is not hard for the youths to find a place near the top of the hill where the brush and trees are dense enough that the ground is more or less dry. They unfasten their tarps and bedding.

The three share with Walter the rations given out by some Japanese and Canadian lodge members and the Lakota Red Cross in the parkinglot of a burned-out mall. Even after eating the four kids are still hungry. Gus feels mildly nauseous. His guts groan. Gus suddenly frowns:

"God-fucking-damnit.... We forgot to buy smoke...."

Maude shrugs. Gus glares at Walter—it's his fault if any-one's. Gladys and Walter are quietly giggling and talking with their heads together.

The wind has returned, moving aside the cloud cover. The night gets cold and everyone adds another layer of clothes. Walter and Gladys get up and sing and shimmy their way through a jumbled medley of four or five current GLOBALSTAR chart-toppers. When they sit down the other two sort of applaud. Walter abruptly says to Gus:

"I wanna, like, come with you, to Lakewood.... Please...."

Gladys grabs Walter and she nods vigorously at Gus and Maude. Gladys makes her pitch:

"He can, like, you know...help me...."

"Do what? Pick out clothes?! Right?"

Maude and Gus laugh. Gladys shakes her head.

"Like, with cooking, and cleaning...."

But Maude is thinking of other things.

"We could get him set up...with documents...."

Gus looks Walter up and down as Maude adds:

"It'd be another full kid's ration. Right?"

"How old are you?"

Walter doesn't answer.

"You gonna be trouble? Huh? Dressing like that?"

"I won't...."

"What about them kids that was chasing you?..."

Walter looks at Gladys. Gladys says:

"He's, like, *my* friend. C'mon, Gus."

She kicks Gus.

"C'mon."

Gus shrugs and smiles at Walter. Walter looks away.

Maude hands Walter a piece of candy and then she hands one to Gus and Gladys. Gus sucks on the cheap hard candy and looks from Walter to Gladys. Maude sits down and then lays back on the bedding.

Maude looks up between the tree foliage up to the sky. Her eyes catch on a satellite tracking across the night sky. Blink blink blink. Far, far overhead. On out of sight, around the earth. As the satellite moves out of her view Maude says:

"He can keep Glad out of our way...."

Gus points his finger at Walter.

"If you and your girlie clothes...get us in any hassles...you're out."

"I won't be, like, any trouble, man."

Walter and Gladys jump up together. Gus reaches out and grabs Walter's leg. Walter stops and looks questioningly. Gus smiles again.

"What are you supposed to say...when someone does something nice for you?..."

Walter hesitates.

"Thank you, Gus."

"That's right."

Maude sits up and says:

"So, why don't you two long-lost sisters take a walk. Right?..."

Gus looks at Maude and smiles. Gladys and Walter look at each other and shake their heads knowingly. Gladys digs her Red Cross–issue wind-up radio out of her satchel. She grabs one of Walter's hands and then says:

"Like, is fucking all there is with you two?"

"Only when we got the time...."

Gus and Maude high-five.

Gus gives the younger two a cigarette each. He holds out his small flashlight and says:

"Emergencies only."

Bert Kaempfert and His Orchestra

As soon as they're out of Gus and Maude's range, Gladys and Walter head right down to the edge of the wooded hill where the park begins and they crouch there in the underbrush. Gladys points to one of the plastimetal park benches.

"Let's sit down."

Walter looks doubtful.

"Gus said not to...."

Gladys looks at him.

"Shit, you only known Gus a few hours...and you already act like he's your...dad, or something...."

"OK, not that bench. One that's...more hid."

Around a bend in the trees there's a plastic bench set back in a screen of pruned bushes. The two kids wipe water off the plastic surface and then Walter spreads his tarp over it. Gladys opens her big parka and she and Walter sit together on the tarp-covered bench inside her big heavy coat. Gladys can pretty much bring the coat closed around them both.

"We'll smoke mine first."

Walter gets his cigarette piece out of an inner pocket. Gladys smiles and says:

"OK. Here. Like, you put this earphone in your ear. Like this. Yeah."

She fits the other small black ear piece in her left ear. Walter lights the cigarette.

Gladys twists the wind-up key in back of the small radio. Fully wound the hand-size set receives for nearly an hour. Tonight, GLOBALSTAR is beaming 24-hours of Pop, Hip-hop and Ranchera down on North and Central America.

The two kids huddle on the bench, arms wrapped around each other, legs raised and tucked up so knees are at chin level. Walter hands off the cigarette as he exhales and asks:

"You from Denver?"

"Yeah. Over near the Arsenal."

"I'm from Indianapolis, Indiana…."

"Shit. Indianapolis."

"I've been in more than twenty cities…. Lived in them."

Gladys gives him a doubting look. Walter purses his lips.

"I can name them…*all*."

"How long you been wearing girls' clothes?"

Walter takes the earphone out of his right ear.

"Why?"

Gladys shrugs. Walter shrugs back and answers with:

"A long time."

They both giggle quietly.

"Why?"

"Huh?"

"Why do you wear girl clothes?"

Walter makes an unsure face.

In that moment a tall very pale caucasian woman strides right up to them. Thick black kohl eyeliner, long straight dark hair pulled back into a loose ponytail. Heavy black leather motorcycle coat, a pullover sweater and faded black jeans tucked into nearly knee-high dirty brown lumberjack boots.

Deep urgent whisper.

"Stevie?…"

No man's voice answers her. Young girl whispering

scared.

"We're just sitting here, lady."

Now a young boy speaks:

"We ain't...seen anybody."

Two kids stand up. The man in the coat, who might have been Stevie, is two kids huddled on the bench in one coat. They separate. Walter slings on his tarp poncho. As the woman realizes her mistake the two kids slink back toward the woods.

"Come back...."

The woman's voice is deep, lush to rough.

Walter slows a bit and looks back at her. The woman gets out an old plastic bandaid box she keeps her cigarettes in and pops the lid and tilts and shakes it toward him. Walter looks at his friend.

"Gladys?..."

Gladys shrugs and grips Walter's right hand. They walk back to the bench.

"You guys smoke?"

The kids nod and keep an eye on this unexpected adult.

The woman's face is broad and pale. Her thick swath of black kohl around her eyes makes her gaze difficult to find.

Gladys and Walter sit on one half of the bench and the woman on the other. Again the woman holds out her plastic bandage box of cheap filterless cigarettes. Gladys fishes out two.

They all light up and look out over the dark park. The cigarettes are so harsh the kids puff on them like they might cigars.

The woman crosses her legs, one booted foot rests on her other leg's knee. She sets her smallish satchel on the bench to her left. A definite smell rises out of the bag.

She looks at the two kids. Both the girl and boy are wearing brightly colored skirts and tops. Both have short buzzed hair.

"My name is Norma...."

"Gladys."

"Walter."

The woman nods and says:

"I knew.... I knew...you were not Steve."

She looks back out over the park.

"I was confused to see anyone else in Winner's Park...at night."

Walter takes a little puff on his cigarette and stares at the woman. Gladys asks:

"You, like, meet your boyfriend here?"

Norma's cigarette stops in mid-motion to her lips. She scowls a little.

"Steve wasn't my boyfriend. We were...in a rocknroll band."

Norma's mind digresses for a moment before she adds.

"But, yes, I used to meet Steve here. When it was a baseball field."

Walter looks around.

"How come, like, they made a baseball field into a...park?"

Norma doesn't answer, her mind has wandered again to better days. Walter prompts her.

"How come?..."

Norma points to the park in front of them.

"Winners."

She points off in the dark toward the identical park in the distance on the north side of the road.

"Heroes."

"Steve was, like, a soldier?"

"Soldier?"

Norma laughs. Low and quiet, more like she is breathing hard. She smokes and looks around the dark park.

93

"No, he was not a soldier."

Norma looks at Walter and Gladys.

"Stevie was picked up by Team Jesus right away. One of the first, right after the Surgical Jesus Mind Project was launched. And pits...are convenient and easy to build. Just dig up a baseball field for instance...."

She looks at the two kids.

"In the beginning, Kingson tried to put a good face on everything, as if no one understood what the Surgical Jesus Mind Project really was. Toward the end, Team Jesus just incinerated most of the heads and corpses and dumped the ashes in the sewers and rivers.... I'm lucky that I know Stevie got buried here."

Norma takes a long drag on her cigarette and exhales a long trail of smoke before going on.

"Once each pit was full of heads and headless corpses tanker trucks were brought in...like for gasoline...and they poured acids and liquid quicklime over the dead.... Followed by truckloads of dirt and gravel."

Norma shrugs.

"Pack down the dirt and gravel. And finally, add new topsoil and sod."

Norma smokes for a moment and then adds:

"The beautiful landscaping...."

Norma takes a drag on her cigarette, the cherry glows brightly and shows her face in dim redness. The cigarette's bright coal jerks away from her lips as Norma points here and there in the darkness.

"Beauty bark where you have trouble getting things to grow."

Norma nods her head and gets out her bandaid box of cigarettes, and lights a fresh cigarette from the butt still smoldering between her deeply nicotine-stained fingers. She holds the box toward the kids, but they are still working on their first ones.

Slowly, and with exacting clarity, Norma repeats:

"Beau...ty...bark.... Beau...ty...bark...."

Norma glances at the children for some sort of confirmation. Gladys and Walter look at each other. Gladys shrugs and says:

"Like...everywhere.... I guess?"

Norma smiles, laughs a little, and then looks at the large man's wristwatch she is wearing.

"I never stay more than a half-hour or so."

"What time is it?"

"Nearly four.... The gardeners show up as early as five...."

"I'm cold, Walter."

"Just a minute, Gladys."

"She's right, it's cold. Let's go to our homes."

Norma stands and looks at the two kids.

"Home? No?"

Norma and the kids shrug in unison. Norma hums some song her band did what seems like many years ago. She starts walking away. Gladys tugs at Walter's poncho. Walter pushes at Gladys and says:

"But, why, like, do you come here, Norma? Every night?"

Norma walks back. She is amused. She opens her poly-canvas satchel. There are a dozen or so bones and bone fragments in the satchel. The stink from the satchel is a heavy sticking-to-the-brain stink. A couple bones gleam white. Most are dirty with bits of corpse clinging to them. There are not enough bones in the satchel for a whole skeleton.

Norma smiles. Gladys and Walter look up from the bag of bones at Norma's face. She smiles again.

"I have to come at night. The gardeners spend the first couple hours of their day scouring for bone and bits.

"Early spring is the best. The freezing and thawing....
Especially after a few days of rain."

She rattles her satchel and looks inside and picks up a small rib, like a child's maybe.

"It's not all Steve, you know...."

Norma looks down at the ground.

"And all that acid...dissolved a lot of the bones...."

Gladys and Walter aren't sure what to say.

Norma scrunches her face negatively.

"The acid-liquefied bone...congeals.... Into pasty-white calcium lumps...."

Norma looks at Walter, he nods.

"I don't pick those...of course.... They crumble. And stink."

Norma wrinkles her nose and sort of rolls the arced rib bone between her fingers. She holds it up. All three strain to study it in the dark.

She plops the bone back into the bag and zips it closed, shrugs and looks at her wristwatch.

"We should all leave."

Done bone searching for the night, Norma pulls off the hair band and shakes out her long dark brown hair as she strides away.

Gladys grabs Walter's hand and they hurry to the woods. As they get close to the trees someone hisses from the underbrush. Gladys and Walter jump and squeak, frightened. Gus pops up and gestures for them.

They get closer and Maude asks:

"Who was that?"

Gladys ignores her question and asks:

"Did you get our stuff?"

Gus throws Gladys the satchel she and Walter now share. Gus is angry and he says:

"I fucking told you...stay out of the park...."

Gladys yawns by way of ignoring Gus. Maude again asks:

"Who was that? What was she selling?"

"Huh?"

"What'd she have in the fucking bag? That she showed you...."

"Nothing...."

Maude glares. Gladys says:

"She wasn't selling nothing."

"She had *something!* I could see that."

This time Walter answers:

"Bones."

Gladys adds:

"People's bones...."

Maude raises her eyebrows as she looks at the two youngest.

"Bones?"

Gus does not believe them.

"People's bones? In the park?"

"There's lots of people buried under these parks. You know, the Surgical Jesus thing...."

Gus points up the wooded hill behind them.

"Like that one up in the hills?"

"No. Buried. In a pit. With no heads. Lots and lots of...."

Gladys looks for a better word. There isn't one.

"People from rocknroll bands...."

"With no heads."

Walter adds. Maude nods, willing to accept that and then she asks:

"But...who is *she?*"

"I think...she's a rock star."

"Yeah, right...."

"No, it's true. A guy from her band is there. You know, buried."

Gus looks out at the park lawn spreading off into the darkness. Gladys yawns and shivers and says:

"I'm tired."

Walter nods.

"Yeah."

Mitch Miller and His Orchestra

This day, these days, late-October, it is already cold. The ten centimeters or so of snow starkly draped over metro Denver give the war-damaged landscape a hallucinatory cleanliness—crystalline and edgy. So what remains here, under this hallucination, of Denver? Fortified patches of money, money's employees, and money's facilities. With no strongman and no political institutions, various factions have launched the state into the current civil war that the Johannesburg ceasefire failed to put a stop to and that is now driving out UNNAA.

Put out your hand. Up. Feel that? Winter is coming. Good and plenty.

Current Red Cross and UNHCR reports calculate that in addition to Colorado's internal refugees there are two to three million refugees from elsewhere compacted, huddled, standing and waiting in the two small UNNAA Protected Zones. One just northeast of metro Denver, in the foothills near Boulder, the other on the plain west of Denver and south of the Rocky Mountain Arsenal.

Several millions more—drug users, unamericans, sodomites, trade unionists, abortionists and satanists all—are on the roads to the UNNAA Protected Zones.

From over here—the castouts of the suburban redneck republic of the Golden West. From over there—refugees from the Shaken East, where still nothing worked, escapees from indentured labor tending hogs or their sewage for Heartland Hog Holdings and the "non–ticket holders" from *ReLive USA!*™

ReLive USA!™ the theme park–entertainment state that Disney and other global culture mobsters cobbled together from the moldering central and southeastern bits of the former United States. The Good Old US of A is back…and shinier! *ReLive USA!*™…. Most of the major stage shows, casinos and rides are concentrated in its "capital", Atlanta.

Tickets and cold drink sales keep the *ReLive USA!*™ government clean and fresh smelling. The real plum is the entertainment state's solid and discreet financial services sector. This gives *ReLive USA!*™ more of an aura of legitimacy than anything else in that part of the continent.

Barry Manilow

Gus is nervous. Not excited. Nervous. Like something bad he has done is about to be exposed. He keeps looking around the remnants of the Lakewood MetroWeb station.... Nervous, expectant.

The station is pretty much intact, despite the neglect of withered bureaucracies. It has been several years since trains regularly pulled into this station on a Friday afternoon like when Gus would detrain here to meet Calvin. The rest of the Rodriguez family would be gone to abuelo's for the weekend. Calvin would be waiting in the family SUV a couple blocks from the Lakewood station. Too many of Calvin's neighbors used the station then for them to meet right out front.

The Lakewood station is not really familiar anymore, but Gus still feels the excitement he used to get.

Gus hurries off toward an exit. Gladys and Walter run after him and Maude grabs one of her boyfriend's satchels to slow him up. He looks at Maude. Maude jumps up and kisses Gus' face. He gives her the eye and smiles and looks back and stops and waits for Gladys and Walter to catch up.

Three white people come toward the kids. A Charity Squad, armed with palm-sized paralyzing aerosol sprays and plastic cuffs. Tall bulky social workers, many of whom used to work for the Surgical Jesus Mind Project, are now employed by one or another of the omnipresent global charities.

Maude flashes open her coat exposing the hilt of her dagger in its sewn-in scabbard. The lead social worker raises her hands and the other two adults stop and the leader holds out a piece of paper.

"You kids know what Great Escape Camps are? It's a *real* chance to *really* get out!"

Woman's eager delivery is distorted by her cold assessment of the four ragged children in front of her and how they can be brought under adult supervision. The four kids keep backing away.

"Not the *maybes* of *trying* to get a sponsor nation or NGO. We've got lots and lots of *big* Jumbo Jets. *And* we've got the money to keep flying kids around the world until we find you homes!"

As she finishes her schtick the four kids assume their defensive formation. The woman looks at Gus. He's the one they have to get rid of to get at the younger three. The lead social worker signals her cohorts. Gus sees this and he rushes the adults, elbows and fists knocking them aside. The four kids head up and over the rubble of the station's collapsed outer walls.

One of the social workers has his paralyzing aerosol in hand, but the team leader shakes her head no.

"We've got our 15 for today. No need to sweat it."

One of the other social workers complains:

"The three young ones would've been a hundred-credit bonus apiece!"

It takes twice as long necessary to for this final leg of their journey, from the MetroWeb station to the cul de sac where the Rodriguezes' house is. Gus has them scramble through gullies and ravines instead of streets. Natural ravines and drainage patterns concreted over during suburbanization to channel waste and runoff from surrounding subdivisions.

These channels are filled with garbage. When it rains, or snow melts, lakes of sewage and water rise behind enormous dams of garbage. Certain low-lying cul de sacs and developments are now toxic swamps and acidic wetlands.

The four kids hurry along well trod narrow trash terraces on the steep embankments. Winding their way among garbage promontories. Trying to keep their noses and mouths covered with rags they'd soaked in water and cigarette butts to try and mask the stink.

The tides of spew and water wash mountains of waste into hillocks and valleys. All along the channels and above on the banks, micro-tribes of salvagers and recyclers live in transient shelters.

Gladys hesitates and stares at neatly sorted stacks of salvage electronic parts. The scavengers of these parts start standing up.

"Jesuschrist, Gladys. C'mon."

Walter tries dragging Gladys, but she is tired and cranky.

Maude grabs Gladys and carries her a few meters. Gladys twists loose and falls into closer step with her companions.

"Cool, look."

Walter points across the channel to where persons unknown have spelled out *666King*, a couple meters high, and a dozen meters along the bank, appliquéd into the trash with children's plastic dolls. A different color scheme of doll for each of the numbers and letters. Some dolls in garments, most not.

Finally, Gus slows and scans the surrounding buildings' silhouettes along the rim of the channel. He recognizes some rooftops. With Walter and Gladys on his right and Maude to his left, the four spider their way up the steep embankment through the brambles and garbage and sharp broken dangerous bits.

The top of the embankment is crowded with Tribber Christians (mostly caucasians) breaking camp and loading up. A few earless Repenters (three white, one black) among them.

It's the earless ones Gus keeps a special eye on. His good eye.

The Christians shout to the four youths.

"Jesus loves you!"

"Come with us to Dallas, the New Jerusalem!"

"Praise the Lord!"

"Spend this Christmas with Jesus!"

"Hallelujah!"

When Gus and Maude flash their daggers the Tribbers halt. One (african american) of the three Repenters reaches inside his coat like he might have a weapon of his own. The other Christians are still trying to interest the kids with promises.

"Plenty of good food at the Second Coming of Our Sweet and Bloody Lord Jesus!"

"No more cold and misery in Dealy Plaza!"

Gus keeps leading the kids forward. Gladys and Walter right behind Gus and right in front of Maude. Small knot of Tribbers follows. Bibles clutched overhead as they trot along, several meters back.

"In one week!"

"Or two!"

"Jesus will be on the Grassy Knoll!"

Maude scoops up a couple baseball-size pieces of rock and broken concrete. She nudges Gus and they smile. Without much windup Maude pitches a well-aimed fastball. Maude beans a caucasian american Repenter with a particularly long list of names on his sash. Right in the forehead, hard. He keels over. Gus laughs, hoots and yells:

"Six six six King!"

Suddenly, from around the corner of a burnt-out house, come another clutch of nasty eager Repenters, some brandishing clubs with nails driven through them. Running, reaching, praying.

One of these Repenters, a white woman armed with a heavy steel spoon encrusted with gore, grasps at Gladys. Gladys flails and yells. Maude smacks the Repenter in the face with a stone. Blood spurts, the Repenter falls backward, dropping her spoon. The Christians stop around their fallen comrades and the kids run on. Some of the Christians pelt the kids with broken things and rocks.

"Children of the Pit!"

"Satan!"

"Carnal spawn of Gehenna! Your time is short!"

"Satan!"

Unable to capture the recalcitrant children the Tribbers stop and vigorously scourge themselves with short lengths of barbed wire.

The four youths leave the Christians and the garbage channels behind and work their way deeper into this subdivision. This part of Lakewood is middle-middle class subdivision origin circa late-1950s.

A dozen or more meters to the kids' far left they hear a pack of feral dogs fighting and barking. The youths stop, listen, and move to stay downwind of the dogs.

The dogs caterwauling, and the death smells involved in that ruckus, has brought around another smaller pack of feral canine domestic companion animals.

The four young humans and this second set of eight or so dogs stop and stare at each other. Several of the descendants of abandoned pets start fierce barking. Some of them are quite large. Gladys and Walter grip Gus' coat tightly. They are restricting his actions so he elbows them.

"Get back...by those trees."

Maude and the two youngest plow ahead through the field grasses toward some trees. Gus follows, facing the dogs. The dogs slowly move in and Gus scoops up a few rocks.

"Maude...."

Maude turns, Gus hands her two halves of sandwiches. Maude pauses and sort of squishes one sandwich half into a ball-form. She tosses it hard enough so it lands among the dogs. The dogs dive for the food. She balls the other half and throws it a little farther away. The dogs chase and gobble that food too. The beasts circle the food ball impact sites, barking or snuffling the ground for more.

"Let's go."

The kids take off. A couple dogs start barking and make to pursue and Maude throws several stones that halfheartedly hit a couple of the canines. The dogs give up pursuit.

The four kids run for several minutes.

They hurry on through a few torched and looted residential subdivisions. Not damaged in the war, but by neighborly looting during times of social chaos. The whole place, including the ground, stinks. Acrid burnt polymers and charred wood.

"Gus, did all these people leave because, like, the armies were, you know, near here?"

"I dunno."

Gladys answers her own question.

"I think so. Maybe two years ago? When that company... I forget who... had those three United States ladies killed?"

Maude retorts.

"They were former First Ladies of the United States. They were trying to get the Reagans to resign. It was Microsoft? Right?"

106

"Whatever. Back then."

They come to a legible street sign. Gladys starts to read the sign aloud, Maude shakes her head no. She looks at Gus. He frowns and says:

"No."

"C'mon, Gus. You gotta practice."

"Just read the fucking sign, Maude."

"You gotta learn to. Right?"

"Fuck you."

Gus steps aside and ponders the two streets that cross at this intersection.

Walter nudges Gladys. Gladys shoves Walter. Gladys frowns and walks over to the sign. She studies it and then says:

"Pioneer Bluff Lane Northwest. And... Pine Cone... Trails.... I think.... Northwest."

Maude shrugs and says:

"But...which is for which direction?"

Out in the middle of the intersection Gus looks up the hill.

Gladys looks around at the looted husks of houses.

"Like, no wonder, no one picked up when you called, Gus."

Walter chuckles. Gladys elbows Walter.

"Their place is probably like that...."

Gladys points to a crumbled burnt shell of a split-level rambler.

"Maybe...."

Gus replies and then he sets off up the steeply inclined street. The street gradually curves away at the crest of the hill, off to the right and out of sight.

Nearer the tops of these foothills the homes are more often intact. Many boarded over, some with just drapes drawn and doors locked. Lawns a couple years overgrown. Shrubs sprawling out over sidewalks. Here and there windows broken, doors forced off hinges. Signs of limited, episodic human habitation.

Highest up the hill, the subdivisions are more or less untouched. Cul de sacs of split-level tombs sealed over with brambles and shrubs amok.

Gus' mood lifts. He slows down. They are getting real close now.

Gus excitedly points to this and that familiar home or street sign. Some truly familiar, others Gus just fancies so. Maude has no interest in this nostalgia. Gladys and Walter stick close together, a couple meters behind the older two. Walter asks Gladys:

"Are these people, like, all dead?...."

Gladys shakes her head no.

"Huh-uh. They all ran off...."

The two youngest look at one particularly spooky run-down house. Gladys thinks about it a moment and adds:

"Now they can't, like, you know, get back...."

Gus is all of a sudden hurrying again. He smiles and points at a house overgrown by shrubs and weeds and he stammers:

"I was...in *that* house. Right there. Calvin had to return a...mulcher...he borrowed after a spring storm."

Gus grabs Maude's shoulder. She shakes off his grip.

"Calvin said I was his nephew. Just like that...*nephew*. And...the guy, he smiled, and shook my hand. Shook my hand."

Gladys rolls her eyes and says:

"Shook your fucking hand.... Jesus."

"Fuck you, bitch. Who shakes your grubby hand."

Maude hits her twitchy partner in the arm as she says:

"Chill out, Gus.... Shit."

Gus looks at Maude.

"Yeah, OK. I'm cool, Maude. I'm cool…."

"Yeah, right."

Gus turns and looks back down the hill. There is Denver. Farther east and south, a horizon of sooty clouds denotes the active status of the military conflict. The battle, having shifted south, has left a horizon of blackened and scarred terrain to the northeast of central Denver.

Gus briefly wonders if his mother, father and two brothers are alive. He turns to the direction he thinks Springfield might be, somewhere in the black clouds of civil war.

Walter sees Gus look back. He sees Gus' moment of question. Walter shrugs and he does not look back. If Walter looked back at Denver it would be all the cities Walter has already fled through in the last few years.

The pallor of smoke and fire. And always now, when it's not overcast, the bloody, bloody red sunsets. Bloody red enough to make you scream.

The purposeful repetition of artillery and rocket bombardments—a project carried out by persons unknown to the kids. Persons as alien now at this great distance, as they are up close, in hand. The sniper's hand.

Gus turns. He is smiling and reaches out both of his hands. Walter jumps to grab Gus' left before Gladys. Maude takes his right. Gladys frowns and then grabs Walter's extended left hand.

Walter sneers and sticks out his tongue at Gladys. He got Gus' hand first. Gladys squeezes Walter's left hand painfully for a moment.

Gus accelerates. The four of them zoom through overgrown early-winter streets. Dust and detritus whip up in their passing.

The New Christy Minstrels

The winding lane narrows between steep embankments. To the kids' left there is a house way up top of the embankment. Like the rest of the neighborhood it is draped in brush and brambles.

As the kids approach the narrowest part of the road, the brush along the left embankment comes alive with animal growls and motion. Cats. Three or four at first. All pretty big. All tensed up for trouble. Backs arced. Ears flattened back. The cats approach the kids turned to their sides, growling low and loud.

Gladys and Walter scream. One of the cats steps back and hisses. The two youngest kids turn and start to run back the way they'd all just come. Gus yells:

"No! Stick right here. Keep together. Behind me."

Gladys and Walter get up close to Gus. Gus and Maude keep slowly moving on ahead, keeping their eyes on the approaching felines. Now there are at least six cats. The underbrush on that side of the road seems full of animals. Cats move out of the bushes and into the road, cutting the youths off from the way they've come.

Maude is staring, fascinated by the cats.

"Here, kitty, kitty."

Cats growl.

Walter's scared voice.

"Look...."

He is pointing up the embankment at the big house

visible way up top. Lots and lots of cats have come out of the house, on to the window ledges and the roof and nearby trees.

Gus is nervous.

"Jesus, Maude. Throw some stones at them!"

Maude stoops, keeping both eyes on the cats, and picks up two fair size pieces of the crumbling road asphalt. She hesitates.

"I like cats...a lot...."

"Goddamnit."

"OK, OK."

The four keep moving on ahead. Maude still hesitates. Maude none too vigorously flings a fist size chunk of road asphalt. The two cats that are in the projectile's trajectory easily leap aside.

The kids keep moving on ahead and a dozen plus cats keep following for a few meters more. But once the kids are well beyond the narrowness in the road the cats begin to back off and retreat up the embankment to their house.

Billy Vaughn and His Orchestra

Maude and Gladys and Walter are hiding in undergrowth near a free-standing garage beside a blue ranch-style house overgrown with brambles.

"Gus is being, like, so weird...."

"Why couldn't we *all* go? Like, no one's gonna be there...."

"Give it a fucking rest...."

Gladys starts to retort. Maude cuts her off.

"Doesn't Gus take care of you two? Right?"

Maude looks from Gladys to Walter. Maude's stare lingers on Walter. She reaches out and slaps Walter's face.

"Huh? Doesn't he?"

Walter's chin is trembling. He manages to say in a steady voice:

"Yes, Maude."

Gladys takes one of Walter's hands and adds:

"We're sorry."

Walter has tears on his face.

Maude frowns.

"Don't be such a crybaby, Walter."

Gladys grips Walter's shoulders as she says:

"We're, just, you know, cold...."

Maude's face twitches and she shakes her head and looks away.

Gus approaches 11256 Mountain Fir Lane through the

backyard. The former backyard. Gus stops and looks around. It is a cold gray day, and except for the periodic overflights of war planes and distant rumbles of bombardments, there are only birds and animals in sight and sound.

Weeds and brambles a meter high cover the big kidney-shaped concrete patio.

Under the second-floor deck, to the left of the sliding glass doors into the daylight basement, Gus sees the large wheeled propane-fired barbecue poking out from the brambles. Nearby is the freestanding shed storing the lawn furniture and other summer equipment. Gus' hands shake. It is cold enough to snow. Sweat rolls down his face. His breath comes out in puffettes of moisture crystals.

Finally he goes back to his friends hiding a block away. All three are cold and cranky. Gus has cleared a trail of sorts to the Rodriguezes'. Once they get to the house they follow its exterior around and up a short embankment to the front.

As the kids approach the big dark wood frontdoor, Gus stops and turns and points to the ground at a patch of concrete barely visible through the plant life and trash.

"See that concrete there? With the pattern on it? That's the sidewalk out to the driveway. It's got that pattern all the way along."

Maude and Walter are unsure of what they're supposed to be seeing. Gladys isn't even looking. She is fascinated with the wrought iron hacienda-style hinges, knocker and handle on the frontdoor. The original frontdoor was more standard; narrower and shorter. It was replaced in the early '70s by this big, beautifully carved, but grossly large and stylistically inappropriate door.

"Are the Rodriguezes, like, medieval, or something?"

Gus looks at the frontdoor of the split-level house.

"I told you, Latino."

Gus points again at the concrete walkway.

"But, look here."

Maude frowns and looks at Gus. He frowns back and points down.

"At the sidewalk."

Now all four of the kids are looking down.

"Those.... that pattern there...is leaves...."

"Leafs."

Gus glares at Gladys.

"The leaves are side by side, all the way to the driveway."

Not one of the three other kids understands. Gus is shifting from exasperated to angry. He speaks slowly.

"When you see the whole walkway...the pattern of leaves...looks like a huge snake...."

The other three look at Gus, the sidewalk and then Gus again. He frowns. Maude jabs him.

"Shit. Don't cry, Gus. Just 'cause we weren't, like, you know...there.... Right?"

Gus shakes his head.

"I'm cool."

Gus turns and heads up the half-dozen cement steps to the frontdoor. Gus has already been inside—he'd jimmied the sliding glass door to the back deck.

To the left of the frontdoor is a meter-wide rectangle of semi-opaque gold-tinted glass that runs up the two floors of the house. In the "old days" (when the electricity was still on) in the evening, the large wrought iron lamp hanging from the second floor over the entryway shone a bright and merry gold.

Inside the entry area the floor is gray slate. Wide, plush-carpeted stairs go up to the main floor. A narrower set off to the left go down to the rec room, laundry and guest rooms.

From the landing at the top of the main stairs you can

choose the family room, the dining room and adjoining kitchen to your right, or to your left, the corridor of bedrooms. A spacious master and two others. What would be a fourth bedroom is converted to the DRESS-UP ROOM. Ramona Barrego Rodriguez had the regular bedroom door removed, the shape of the doorway arched and widened, and a fancy lockable wrought iron gate installed. This gated DRESS-UP ROOM became the repository for the family iconography, photographs and alleged heirloom furniture.

Among the alleged is a smallish baroque couch, reputedly Castilian and 300 years old. But the room's centerpiece is a dark wood sideboard with blackened iron hinges and locks and intricate hand engraving from late-Porfirista Mexico. Its shelves and counter are covered with all manner of Rodriguez and Barrego framed family photos. The central theme of these photos is the son, Davy Rodriguez.

At one end of the room, behind the main furniture setting, a tall chifforobe holds Ramona's designer evening wear.

At the other end of the room is an array of religious objects and saint icons at the center of which is a 1.3 meter high plaster icon of Our Lady of Guadeloupe. Brought north in the 1940s when grandfather Barrego immigrated to Denver and started a small accounting firm.

The firm's success moved the Barregos up the relatively race-friendly class ladder of the immediate post-WWII years. Right on up into the mostly caucasian suburb of Lakewood. And there, 20 years ago, Calvin Rodriguez married into the family and accounting firm, and helped generate Davy.

Gladys and Walter grab the iron gate of the gewgaw sanctuary and shove and shake it in unison. The gate is firmly in place. The two stop and peer inside the DRESS-UP ROOM.

They cannot really see much. The room is dark. The once-special room is now a haven for rodents.

Gus steps from the kitchen into the hall. The kids at the iron gate turn and look at him. Gus jangles a handful of keys on a couple interlocking rings. When Gus gets to the gate he says:

"This room is dress up only."

Walter, face pressed to the bars, asks:

"Why?"

Gus is testing the keys in the lock, and by way of answer he says:

"Christ. You know.... Special Occasions...."

A key goes in, but does not turn. He tests more keys.

"A holiday, abuelo's birthday, someone in the family dies...."

Finally a key turns smooth and the lock clicks open. Walter and Gladys release their grips and the wrought iron gate swings inward.

The room is dim behind the drawn remnants of translucent acrylic drapes. The once-plush white satin settee and chairs are a blotched gray and lounged on now only by rodentia.

"This whole house, like, *smells*. This room...is real bad."

"Mice shit."

"Great."

Gus yanks at the dirty white curtains and they tear apart more than slide open. Maude is a little gentler and the other window curtains slide apart. The outdoor light is not strong enough to add much contrast to the room's topography.

Gus walks over to the holy end of the room. He finds the wall socket he's looking for and plugs in a strand of small blue xmas lights. Of course nothing happens. He stands up and looks around at the room.

Maude is doing a thorough thief's-search of the room.

116

Looking inside, under and behind. She sees Gus staring at the unlit xmas lights and scoffs:

"You...are severely brain damaged...."

Gus ignores her and says:

"You gotta see this room with the colored lights on. It's cool."

Walter and Gladys are fiddling with the latch to the chifforobe.

"Like, what's in here, Gus?"

"Ramona's good dresses. I don't think any of them'll fit either of you...."

Walter and Gladys yank open the doors and three mice dash out and the kids jump back. In plastic clothes bags are some rather dowdy gowns. All too big for either of the disappointed and rodent-nervous kids.

Walter and Gladys walk over to the display of family photos centered around the Rodriguez son, Davy.

"Which is, you know, Calvin?"

Gus comes over and picks up a photo of Calvin, Ramona, Davy, Barbara and Tina from a few years ago, wipes the glass with his palm and points out Calvin. Gladys pokes Walter.

"Duh, Walter. Of course...it's *that* guy."

"Fuck you."

Gus points to the boy in a big solo portrait at the center of the display.

"That's Davy."

Walter stares at the group photo. He asks:

"Wow, like, how old is the youngest girl, Gus?"

Gus looks at where Walter's finger points.

"Tina? Your age...a little older."

Walter grabs Gladys.

"Our age...our size...."

"Gus! Where's Tina's room?!"

"The bedroom just before the stairs. First bedroom on the right."

Gladys and Walter tear out of the DRESS-UP ROOM. Walter careens through a string of spiderweb. He screams and flails his arms about. Gladys grips her friend and reassures him there's no spiders on him. They proceed on more cautiously.

The bedroom end of the house is a square attached to the rectangle of the rest of the split-level rambler. Master bedroom is twice as big as the others. It runs corner to corner on one side. The favored son inhabited the better of the other two bedrooms. And until Barbara moved out, the two Rodriguez girls had to share the remaining corner bedroom.

Mouse encounter forgotten in their fashion frenzy, Gladys and Walter yank open one side of the room's closet. The clothes in this side of the closet are too big. Gladys impatiently yanks open the door on other side of the closet. Aaah. Eager hands dive in.

The two kids turn on the chest-of-drawers and yank out clothes in heaps.

"No! That's, like…my color. I get to try it on first."

"Fuck you."

Gladys releases the pullover and starts grabbing other things in any of her favorite colors.

Gus and Maude are standing at the door to the former bedroom of the Rodriguez girls watching Gladys and Walter. Maude laughs at their frenzy.

"Looter's Christmas."

Gus isn't paying attention, he sees a blue jacket hanging in the closet and he remembers seeing Barbara in it. The jacket gets him thinking about his last encounter with Calvin, a little over four years ago.

The Ray Conniff Singers

The speed has worn off. Gus is hungry and he hasn't slept in a few days and he looks it. He paces and waits in the parkinglot outside the Rodriguez family's favorite seafood restaurant.

As the Rodriguezes leave the restaurant Gus walks right up to the five of them and stops right in front of them.

"Hi, Calvin."

No one replies. Moment of sharp-as-broken-glass silence.

The three Rodriguez children stare at Gus. Mrs. Rodriguez turns away, refusing to look at Gus. Like she is facing away from a car crash or shit on the sidewalk.

Gus' jaw works but no more words come out. He looks away. He does not ask for the hundred dollars he was going to demand.

The Rodriguez family walks on by. Oldest daughter Barbara turns, and she and Gus study each other a moment. Barbara is wearing the blue jacket. Gus shifts his satchel on his shoulder and walks away.

A year ago, while living in a warehouse squat, Maude and Gus worked odd-jobs for beer and food at a speakeasy. One night Gus was being a bouncer and the older Rodriguez daughter, Barbara, came in with several other young women. The aisle from Barbara's table to the bar leads right near Gus. She is the one that goes to the bar for her and her friends' first round. Gus tries very hard to disappear into the shadows. But Barbara recognizes Gus. Even so, she only breaks stride a bit.

Gus watches Barbara walk on to the bar. He decides to speak to her on her return passage to her table.

A few minutes later as Barbara returns bearing drinks, Gus starts to step forward and speak, but Barbara distinctly turns her head. He stops. She passes by. Gus blushes and openly leers after her, making sucking noises with his puckered lips. Barbara ignores him. Gus forces himself to laugh as loud as he can.

Nelson Riddle and His Orchestra

"Shit! There's holes in most of these sweaters!"

Walter angrily throws several moth-eaten wool sweaters to the floor.

Gus takes Maude's hand. She nods down the hall toward the master bedroom.

The master bedroom is very big. The master bed is huge; West Coast King-size it's called. Gus puts his satchel on it and takes off his coat. Maude does the same.

"Did, like, you and Calvin…do it…on this bed? *And* his wife and him? Cool. It's so…TV."

Gus kicks at the bed. No rodent activity. He jumps on the bed. No rodent activity. Gus spreads his big, lined parka across the discolored blue satin bed spread, lining-side up. They spread a few blankets over the open coat.

Maude closes the master bedroom door, sheds her outer layers of clothes, and gets between the blankets and the coat. After Gus has stripped to his last layer of long johns he joins her. The sunset sky outside the master bedroom windows catches his eye. It is so red that for a moment he panics thinking there is a fire.

"Shit. Check out the cool sunset."

Pink overhead, deepening to the western edge of the earth, where the Rocky Mountains hunch in dark blood.

Kitty-korner across the hall, the younger two are now careening through all possible outfit combos from Tina's and

121

some of Barbara's clothes.

"Crappy colors."

Walter looks at what he has on and answers:

"I like the greens...and blues."

Gladys is matching up garments in sets, side by side on the floor. She says:

"Tina couldn't have taken too much with her. I mean, when the Rodriguezes left...."

Gladys points at the closet and dresser, both now despoiled of mounds of girl clothes.

"There's so much here...."

"She probably had lots more."

An hour or so later, Maude and Gus come out of the master bedroom because they hear a hard hammering against a nearby wall. They find Walter and Gladys in the DRESS-UP ROOM, both are wearing Tina's clothes, and wacking a wall with sticks.

Gus frowns.

"What's up?"

Gladys answers between whacks.

"People like the Rodriguezes...they had to have a safe.... They gotta. Probably in here, right?"

Walter hits the wall with renewed vigor. Gus reaches over and stops him.

"No, it's not in here."

Walter and Gladys freeze. They laugh and high-five.

"I told you!..."

Gladys steps back and looks at Maude and Gus.

"You were gonna hide that?"

Gladys punches Gus.

"You guys, were like, gonna get the treasure...and leave us!"

"Don't be stupid.... We were not...."

Downstairs in Calvin's den Gus feels along the wood molding in one corner. When he gets the right spot Gus gently pries off a section of molding and sets it aside. He pulls the exposed carpet edge and rolls it back a couple meters. There is a square cut into the wood floor. Gus plucks up the square of false floor. Below that is the steel door of a safe.

"Calvin said he put this in one summer when his kids and wife were away on vacation."

"You mean…his wife don't know?"

"Huh-uh."

Gladys looks at the safe, its dial and lever. Gladys shakes her head no.

"This isn't electronic…. I don't know nothing about tumblers and dials and shit."

Gus looks at the safe's door. The door's metal is probably not that thick. With a pick and an hour he could probably batter his way in…but what would survive the attack? There's the usual spread of home tools. But no electricity means hand tools only. Maude taps her boot toe on the wood floorboards.

"He's gotta have a drill in that shop downstairs, right?"

"You got some electricity we can run it on?"

"Hand drill…."

Gus nods. Walter suggests:

"We could shoot lots of holes in it."

Gladys shakes her head.

"And what's in there gets fucked up."

Walter pushes Gladys and retorts:

"Not if we just shoot the edges."

Gladys laughs. Walter purses his lips. Gus shakes his head.

"I'm not gonna shoot holes in the fucking safe, Walter."

Maude gets an idea.

"Gus, was it all steel…on the inside?"

"Only the door is metal…."

"So, the bottom is wood. Right?"

Gus nods. Maude adds:

"Wood'll be a lot easier to cut and drill through. Right?"

As far as they can figure it, the bottom of the safe should be in the ceiling of the basement family room. Gus holds the ladder while Maude starts probing for the bottom of the safe. First with an awl and then a screwdriver. Maude takes a crowbar, and wearing ski goggles, she smashes a hole through the spackled ceiling board.

There between two floor beams is a square of thick oak that is the safe bottom.

"Yeah…it's wood on the bottom here…."

"Hey, listen…. That oak bottom piece is gonna be harder to get through than these pine beams…."

Gus shrugs.

"So….We go in from the side. Right?"

Gus and Maude high-five. Gus takes the hand drill up the ladder. Maude grips the ladder to steady it and says:

"Do what you can. I'll spell you."

When there are two holes drilled into the pine floor beam so they overlap one another a bit, Maude sets to careful work with a small narrow saw.

Gus is drawing and pushing the saw when the safe is finally broached. The small section of the beam they are working on is fully cut out and drops and hits the carpeted basement floor.

Gladys and Walter cheer and do a few dance steps. Gus gets down. Maude scurries up. Her hands are smaller. Maude pops her hand inside the safe and draws out several manila envelopes. One envelope is full of small denomination former United States Savings Bonds. There is very little folding money. A hundred dollars or so in former United States greenbacks.

"That's all...for all that work?"

"There...used to be...Calvin's small metal lockbox in there."

Maude sticks a hand back inside and rummages. Her face lights up. She draws her hand back, but the metal box is too big to fit through the opening they've cut.

"Oh, shit."

She lets go of the box.

"I am not cutting out more of that beam."

"I'm hungry...."

Walter pokes Gladys. She ignores him and complains again:

"You guys have been doing this all day...."

Maude glares at her and Gus says:

"Canned food in the pantry."

"I thought...the Rodriguezes would have, like, you know...Mexican food...."

Gus shrugs. Maude says:

"You know how to work a can opener? Right?"

Gladys stands up.

"Fuck you."

"Leave the instant cereal and Malt-o-Meal for me."

"Gus and his fucking *delicate* stomach."

Gladys and Walter go off to rifle the canned food supply.

Gus picks up the crowbar.

"We'll push the box to the far side, across from the hole. I'll put the edge of this..."

Gus hefts the crowbar.

"...against the lock, and pound with the hammer?..."

"Gimme the gloves. I'll try and steady the bar. Right?"

125

Maude holds firm on the crowbar and looks away as Gus swings heavily at the flat, hooked end. He hits it again, and once more. Maude yells:

"OK, OK."

Gus draws out the crowbar. Maude yanks off a glove and stuffs the same hand back in the safe and fingers through Calvin Rodriguez's now-broken lockbox.

Several small black plastic film containers. Two of the film containers hold very dry marijuana. The third an undeveloped roll of film, marked "GF, RD and JLK".

Gus stares at Calvin's neat printing.

Sets of documents for two bank accounts in Calvin's name alone. Three credit cards, in Calvin's name. Expiration date a year or more past.

There is some cash in the metal box. Several hundred former United States Dollars. Similar amounts of Yen and original-issue red Golden West Credits (from back when the Golden West states were still more of a vast gated community than a larval nation-state).

"I'm surprised he didn't take this stuff with him."

Gus shrugs.

"I bet he woulda if he'd had a chance."

There is also a zip-lock baggie with a few condoms and a small tube of lubricant zipped inside. Maude examines them.

"Way expired."

There are two small sealed white envelopes with keys in them. And three larger envelopes that each hold between 10 and 20 snapshot photos. On the front of the envelopes are sets of two or three letters carefully penciled on the envelope.

Gus looks at the envelopes. The different sets of initials. Gus holds up one of the envelopes. He looks at Maude. His face is passive, but his hands tremble some.

Without even undoing the rubber band, or looking at the photos in that particular envelope, Gus hands the envelope to Maude.

Maude keeps her hands in her jeans pockets and looks at the envelope in Gus' hand.

"What's in there, Gus?"

"Photos."

Maude looks at Gus.

"Yeah? Of you?"

"I dunno."

"Fuck you don't."

Maude steps back and smirks and says:

"I don't wanna see more Rodriguez family photos...."

Gus slips off the rubberband and flips open the chosen envelope's flap. Pause. He pulls out the stack of snapshots and looks at the top photo a moment and then rifles through the rest until two certain photos turn up.

Gus looks at the two photos a minute.

Maude sees Gus flush and his face contort. Gus tries to letter-by-letter sound out the notes on the back of each photo. He looks up and sort of grins.

"These two are me...."

Gus' strange glittery smile. Maude takes the two snapshots and holds one in each hand. After a moment of looking from one photo to the other Maude starts laughing. She punches Gus in the gut, playfully. Gus smiles uneasily. She tries to see the rest of the photos.

"What are the rest? More you and Calvin?"

Gus isn't smiling.

"No.... Just other guys."

Maude raises an eyebrow.

"Other guys? What's up? I mean.... You and Calvin—man and wife forever?... Right?"

Maude takes the 14 photos from Gus' reluctant hand.

Calvin Rodriguez fucking teenaged boys. She scrutinizes them all, but returns to the two photos of Gus and Calvin.

"How come I never see you that cranked off?"

Gus grimaces.

"I was mugging for the camera."

Maude chuckles and looks at a few other photos.

"Calvin is even uglier naked. Right?"

"C'mon. Give'em back."

"I like seeing you…different from how I see you…."

Gus blushes. Maude smiles.

"And you being so young…."

Gus stuffs the photos in a coat pocket and smiles slyly.

"I bet we can trade these…. Like we did those others."

Maude laughs and Gus asks:

"Where's the smoke?"

"There. Did Ramona smoke weed too?"

"Naw…."

Maude shakes her head and heads for the kitchen.

"Let's drink those beers we found in the basement fridge. We can turn one of the cans into a bong. Right?"

Gus and Maude find the other two kids eating a plastican of fruit cocktail. Gus shakes one of the little containers of marijuana.

"We found some smoke in the safe!"

"Yeah!"

"What else was in the safe?!"

Maude shrugs and mundanely says:

"Some money…stupid business papers…part of a dead baby…."

Gladys stops chewing the soft syrupy sweet fruit cubes. Walter says:

"Which part?"

Gladys smiles and adds:

128

"Which baby?"

Walter hoots loudly.

Maude goes over to the sliding glass door to the deck, slides it open some and brings in the box of beers. The beer is nicely cold.

Maude hands one of the 400ml cans to Gus. He snaps the OPEN tab, tilts the can back and downs it all. Maude takes a couple sips of hers. When his beer is empty Gus pauses, breathes, wipes his lips, tilts the can back again for any remaining dribbles and then belches and announces:

"OK. Let's get high."

Using his thumbs and fingers Gus crimps and crumples a little pocket into one side of the aluminum beer can. A few jabs of a safety pin into the crimped pocket and Gus has a working water pipe.

"Get the jug of water we bottled. I don't want us sucking up any sick water. And give me that other beer."

Maude hands her partner the third of the three beers. Gladys frowns.

"What do we get?"

"I need more I'm bigger."

"Gus' stomach is delicate so he gets the oatmeal.... Gus is bigger so he gets two of the fucking beers."

"You'll be getting stoned in a minute. Right?"

Even though the cannabis at hand is a couple years old, its effect on Walter is to prostrate him on the couch after only two tokes. It has an opposite effect on Gladys, her blood sugar level shoots through the roof and she is off and going.

"Hey, Can we, like, drag the lady statue...into our room?"

Gus thinks about it.

"Huh, Gus?"

Gus shrugs.

"Will you help us, Gus?"

Gus frowns and Gladys pleads:

"It's, like, way too heavy for us...."

"So? Do *I* want it in *your* room?"

"C'mon, Gus...."

"No!..."

Gus glares at Gladys. She sighs.

"OK, whatever. Can we, like, use your flashlight?"

Gus points to the dining table and the flashlight on it. A blackened iron chandelier over the table is draped in dust and webs.

"C'mon, Walter."

"Be careful...."

More impatient.

"C'mon, Walter. Get up."

"Let him lie."

Walter manages to sit up. Squinting bloodshot eyes. Walter swallows.

"Shit. I'm thirsty."

Gladys giggles and heads off skipping to their bedroom. Walter sort of crawls after her.

Gus and Maude are sharpening their daggers. Even over the rasp rasp rasp of one edge of a blade at a time back and forth on the spit stone, the older two can hear the younger two in the DRESS-UP ROOM straining and struggling with the statue. Cursing and complaining.

It is a couple minutes before Gladys and Walter and the plaster icon even make it into the hall. Gladys pulling the icon from under the arms and Walter pushing at Mary's pedestal.

Maude sits up some so she can see the toilers better.

"They might do it...."

But Gladys collapses and after a moment of huffing and puffing calls out:

130

"Gus! We *really* can't, like, get it…*any* farther…."

"Please, please, Gus."

Gus grins and yells out.

"Sorry, I'm busy now…eating Maude's pussy!…"

Maude kicks Gus as he laughs.

"What? C'mon, I could be…."

"Don't make fun of eating my pussy, dickbrain. Right?"

Maude kicks Gus again.

"C'mon, I wasn't…."

"You're the hog for it."

Gus snorts a couple times. Maude points down the hall and says:

"You're the fucking o-sumo-san. Right?"

"Oh, Christ…."

"One of them's gonna start crying…."

"Alright."

Gus gets up and stretches. Maude rubs her stomach.

"I wish the oven worked. I'd bake cookies. I got crazy munchies."

Gus stops, reminded.

"You said you were going over to the house next door to get more better food…."

"Get that statue into their room, then maybe I'll go search a few of those houses."

Gus carries the Mary icon into what is now Walter and Gladys' room. Walter flops on the bed. Gus gets the icon set up and steady on top of the dresser drawers.

Gladys follows Gus back out to Maude in the living-groom. She says:

"Gus says you're going next door for cookies. I wanna go too."

"I didn't say anything about being able to get cookies. Right?"

Gus laughs, Maude punches him.

"Asshole."

Gladys pleads. "I wanna go with you...next door...."

"Get your coat and boots."

"I wanna have all the chocolate syrup they have in those houses."

"Just the two next door. Right?"

"Are there gonna be dogs? Nice ones? We could have a pet."

Maude ignores Gladys and says to Gus:

"Where's Walter?"

"Crashed out."

Maude points to Gladys.

"Don't you ever get these two..."

And then she points down the hall.

"... this high again. Right?"

"Maude? Maude, I want to, like, find a Ericsson-Honda laptop."

"Shut up."

"In one of these houses."

Gus grabs Gladys and presses his palm over her mouth. She kicks him and twists loose. Gladys glares silently. Gus shrugs at Maude.

"I didn't think it'd still be so strong. Must be, close to three years old?..."

Gladys interrupts:

"They wouldn't, like, take all their computers, huh? Not like their...*big* ones at least. Right? You think, Maude?"

"Shut up. Or you're not going with me."

Gus shoves Gladys toward the frontdoor. Gus hands Maude the flashlight.

"Aren't you coming?"

"I'm gonna look for some of the Christmas decorations."

132

"You'll need the flashlight."

"I'm...pretty sure there's...a flashlight here.... In the shop. Down in the basement...."

Maude shrugs.

For a couple minutes Gus stands in front of the big living-groom picture window and watches the two girls' slow progress to next door. Dark winter overcast sky.

Once the two girls go into the neighboring house and don't leave immediately, Gus steps back from the window. He looks down the dark hall toward the bedrooms.

From the room Gladys and Walter live in, dim flickering light of candles barely washes into the hall.

Gus steps out of his boots and treads softly to the gently illuminated doorway.

Difficult to see inside the room at first. There are four candles set in a large metal jar lid on the floor.

Girl clothes are spewed everywhere.

Walter is there under some blankets on a bed. The plane of light from the candles on the floor is cut at a sharp angle by the bed's edge and only a hint of the light touches a bit of Walter's face and hair.

Arthur Fiedler and the Boston Pops

"Merry Christmas!"

And then.

"C'mon, look!"

"Look at this, Gus!"

Gus and Maude are asleep in their bedding piled on the master bed. Walter steps up to the head of the bed and holds out two large glass Christmas tree ornaments.

"We found the rest of the Christmas stuff, Gus!"

"And the bottom half of the plastic tree!"

Maude sticks her head out from under the bedding into the cold morning. She stares at the red and blue glass orbs delicately styled in holiday patterns. She croaks:

"So?"

Gladys and Walter look at each other with near disbelief.

"Gus has got to get up so he can get the tree set up. Jesus…."

Maude shakes her head in disbelief and says:

"Fuck the plastic tree. He's gotta go get the barbecue going for hot water for coffee."

Gladys complains:

"What are we gonna have for breakfast?"

Walter chimes in:

"That cereal had bugs in it."

"Just the one box."

Gladys scowls at Maude's flippancy about bugs. Gus starts shifting and stretching under the layers of blankets. He gropes up, out of the bedding. He pulls on a torn T-shirt and two wool shirts. Finally Gus looks at Walter standing there beside the bed. Eager smile and a big Christmas ornament in each hand.

Gladys raises the ornaments above her head, Walter follows suit, and Gladys says:

"Walter is a loser!"

Gladys laughs at Walter. Walter lowers his arms and says:

"You're a retard sometimes, Gladys Picker."

Gladys shoves Walter and he lurches to one side. He angrily responds:

"Picker? What sorta name's Picker? Nose picker."

Gladys punches him and Walter yells:

"Peckerwood, more like."

"Fuck you. You're as white as I am. You just like to say you're part black."

"I am too. Mom's side of the family...."

"Your mom...."

"Shut up."

They glare at each other. Gladys changes subjects.

"We can make hair for the statue out of the tinsel."

An hour later, in the livingroom, they are all four engrossed in what they dig out of the Christmas decoration boxes. Gus looks over at what Maude is doing.

"No, listen...the nativity scene has to go over by the fireplace. Move the fireplace tools."

Maude is playing with figures from the Rodriguez family crèche. Handcrafted wood figures and manger structure, painted deep bright colors. Purchased in Mexico City while the family was there for the 1968 Olympics.

Maude has the animals set up to feed from a mound she has made with a bunch of silver and blue-silver tinsel.

"The tinsel is supposed to be around the family photos

135

over there.... And there's s'posed to be some lights on the wall behind the photos."

Gus leans forward and after a moment's search points to a couple small holes in the wall.

"There's the holes that the nails are supposed to go in."

Maude glances at where Gus is pointing. She shakes her head, irritated.

"I don't care, Gus. If I'm gonna have fun, I gotta play with 'em. Right?"

He frowns.

"It's Christmas. Not...playing."

Maude deploys the Wise Men and Shepherds inside the manger area. She arrays the bits of railing between them and the Holy Family. She takes the donkey and slowly cavorts the small wooden figure across the path of the Holy Family. Evil, squeaky voice:

"La-la-la. I'm a little burro, shitting shitting shitting, all the places you stupid God people gotta go across. Have a nice day. La-la-la."

Gus frowns again and says:

"You, like, think you're so smart...but you're not...."

Gus has loaded the turntable of the immense hi-fi/TV console with a stack of five Christmas LPs. Henry Mancini, Percy Faith, and Burt Bacharach—each with his Orchestra and chorus—and two of Herb Alpert and the Tijuana Brass' Christmas albums are all in this special holiday mix. Gus has the bass and volume knobs cranked up. He presses PLAY. The old wood cabinet is silent and dark. The records do not play their easy cheerful Holiday tunes. Gus wills the electricity to flow. It does not.

Running out of his and Gladys' bedroom Walter swoops into the front room wearing a blue dress, with a blue shawl and then a white shawl over the blue shawl, both covering his head. The shawls drape over his shoulders, front and back.

Gladys follows Walter. She is holding a family photo album looted from a house next door. Gladys says:

"Walter thinks he's Nuestra Señora...."

The other three watch as Walter spins around a couple times. He does a saucy little dance.

"The Holy Mother never did dances like that. Right?"

"And that statue lady is nearly black skinned."

"And you are all white, Walter."

Gladys laughs and Walter scowls. Maude laughs, and leans over and pinches Walter's face. Maude watches the redness on Walter's skin from her pinch.

"Yup, white."

"But, like...if I spend more time in the sun...."

The other three look unconvinced.

"A lot...more...."

He looks at Maude and Gus, pleading.

"Then, like, I'd be as brown as Her. Right, Gus?"

"Maybe."

Maude laughs.

"You're a sad little fuck, Walter. You're a boy that wears girl's clothes, right? *And* a white boy that wants to be black. Right?"

Gladys shakes her head knowingly and says:

"Walter's *always* saying he's as black as you, Maude...."

Walter scowls. Gladys sticks her tongue out at him and then she says:

"Yesterday Walter said he's pregnant.... *And* that he can *feel* the baby...in his belly."

Gus gawks at Walter and then laughs. Walter glares at Gus and then hangs his head down, dejected. Maude stands up and stretches and says:

"I'm gonna go look through the next two or three houses."

Maude gets her coat and the flashlight. Gladys drops the photo album she's scrutinizing onto the couch and grabs her own coat off the coffee table.

"I'm coming. I want to get some more, like, of these family photo albums."

Maude ignores her and asks Gus.

"Where's the blue satchel I brought back last time?"

Gus points toward the kitchen.

"By the fridge."

Gus looks at the artificial Christmas tree and the ornaments and the tinsel. He's hung his ornament at the front of the tree, instead of the back and down low like Calvin used to. But the festive music and the flashing lights are what's really missing.

Walter is still standing on the coffee table, all dressed up like the Mother of God. He lifts his raiments and starts getting down off the low table.

"Wait, I'll change."

"I'm not waiting."

Maude heads to the frontdoor.

Walter whines.

"It won't take me long…."

He runs down to the hall to his and Gladys' bedroom. Maude trots downstairs to the frontdoor and yells back up:

"Catch up with us…."

Gladys runs down the steps after Maude.

Walter's plaintive voice from the bedroom:

"Glad! Wait for me…."

Gladys yells up from the frontdoor:

"Maude's got the flashlight!"

Walter's angry shout:

"Fuck you…."

The frontdoor slams close behind Gladys.

138

Sting

"No...."

Walter says the word more insistently.

"No."

Walter is not looking at Gus. Walter has shed his Nuestra Señora drag for regular girl clothes. Gus' grip nearly fits around Walter's leg. His big hand is strong and persistent, squeezing and massaging the inside of the boy's leg, far up under his skirt.

"I don't wanna, Gus...."

"What is it...honey?"

Gus leans closer to Walter. Walter jumps up from the red velveteen couch in the livingroom that he and Gus are sitting on.

"No."

"C'mon, sweetie."

Gus keeps his voice quiet and deep, but it is at least as insistent as Walter's.

"What? I've been taking care of you. Right? Now...you can give me that special kiss.... You know."

Walter looks mad.

"I thought...I was supposed to.... I thought...Gladys was too."

Gus smirks.

"Nothing like that."

Walter glares.

"You're a liar, Gus."

Walter wants to strike out, but the steady pressure of Gus' pawing hand reminds the boy of the strength of the near-man. Walter, frustrated, folds his arms and says:

"You leave Gladys alone...too. Both of us."

"Nobody is touching Gladys."

Walter doesn't believe it.

"I don't think Maude would like it."

Suddenly Gus has his dagger firmly in hand. Gus is not pointing it at Walter, but Gus is angry, threatened. He twists the dagger so the blade flashes sharply.

"You talk to Maude...and I'll cut you open. Top to bottom."

Walter steps back.

"I wasn't gonna. I just said...."

Gus re-sheathes his dagger, smiles and reaches out for Walter.

"I know, baby. Come here. Just be nice."

Gus takes Walter's hands in his and draws him closer. The younger boy stands there in front of Gus. Who remains seated.

"Just be nice, Walter. All I want is that special kiss."

Gus runs his hands up under Walter's wool skirt and violently gropes his ass. The boy squeals.

"Walter.... We discussed you and screaming."

"I'm sorry, Gus.... I...get...nervous."

The two males look at each other. Walter relaxes, Gus gives a bit on his grip, Walter relaxes more. Gus smiles and straightens the younger boy's clothes. Walter looks at Gus.

The Ray Charles Singers

Gladys and Walter are set up on the couch thumbing through the four new photo albums Gladys scavenged from neighboring houses. Maude and Gus are in the kitchen scrutinizing the few firearms Maude has scavenged from nearby houses. The weapons and ammunition and accessories are laid out on the kitchen table. Maude is perturbed.

"I can't, like, believe *everyone* took all their good guns."

"Kingson made a lot of places force-collect guns."

"I was sure we'd, like, find a nice little automatic something. With spare clips. Right?"

Gus shrugs at Maude's whole interest in firearms. Maude again picks up a small plastimetal .32 caliber semi-automatic pistol. With its two-inch barrel and stocky magazine, the pistol has a square profile. Gus shakes his head.

"Just because it's almost plastic…doesn't mean some checkpoint scanner thing won't identify it as a gun."

"All the time they see we got daggers…. Right?"

"Kids with, like, knives…is different."

"So…."

Gus restrains his irritation.

"What are you gonna do when they stop you?"

Gus glares at Maude.

"Shoot it out with 'em?"

Gus grabs up one of the other guns, an older, former United States military-issue revolver.

"What about us, Maude?"

Maude scowls. Gus continues:

"They'll put you on one of those Charity jets and fly

you off to…slavery…or somewhere…."

"We never go through places that tight…."

"All I got to say is….What are the rest of us gonna do?"

"I can get shot everyday. Right? What's this gonna change?"

"Fuck you."

"We could get a lot for any of these guns…back in Denver…."

Gus shakes his head and looks away and says:

"You carry it. Not me. Ever."

"Yes. Whatever, Gus…."

Gus stretches and gently touches his stomach. His stomach has been off-and-on yucky all day. Everyday for the last week, seems like.

The String-A-Longs

Maude sucks on the last of a cigarette and looks at Gus.

"This whole thing here is...really getting boring, Gus."

Gus doesn't get it. Maude takes the fresh cigarette he just lit and puffs and draws the smoke back up through her nostrils.

"This place ain't some Heaven. It's cold and it smells. And I heard differently about Heaven. Right?"

Gus doesn't like it said, even if he agrees. He frowns and remains silent. Maude gets irritated at his stubbornness and she takes a different, ruder tack.

"In Heaven Calvin Rodriguez fucked you...for a xmas ornament.... Right?"

This Gus actively protests.

"But, it wasn't...."

Gus' hands grope in the air unable to find words.

"I never.... That sex...was nothing.... Really...."

He looks at Maude and frowns.

"Calvin never...asked me...for anything...."

"Jesus-fucking-Christ. That is some *severely* pathetic bullshit, Gus."

"No."

Gus folds his arms across his chest. He tries to be proud of himself and Calvin. He flashes on a certain day; Calvin and him on the back deck in the sun. He remembers the promises and more promises. Calvin loved to promise; it generated a tenderness in his heart that made him horny. Gus frowns and then looks at Maude.

He waves his hands again. More frantic, upper lip damp.

"You can look back, on anything, and see just the…bad stuff…."

"I'm not saying Rodriguez didn't do things for you. Right?"

"He let me just…be here…. Like…. Like *I* lived here…."

Maude shrugs.

"This house is OK…."

Gus stands up and looks at the wreck they've already made.

"The house is not, OK…. Without them…the Rodriguezes… living their lives…."

Gus is at a loss for words.

"It doesn't have…much…of their clean smell."

He points to the livingroom floor. Now dark and dirty.

"While I was doggin' it…. I could smell how clean this place was. Their lives smelled so clean."

Gus' voice is unsure. He looks around again.

"Let's torch it, Maude. Maybe, it'll burn the whole neighborhood."

She smiles. "Too wet…I think."

"No way…."

Walter's voice collapses. Gladys picks up the complaint.

"Burn our house down?…"

Gladys looks at Walter. He is open-mouth-hopeless. Gladys turns back to the older two.

"But, like, we got a nice place here…."

Maude gestures around.

"C'mon, we've used it up here. Right?"

Gus laughs and says:

"We'll do it *666King*-style."

Tears streak Walter's face, his lips tremble. Maude takes his arm.

144

"Not today, honey. Tomorrow. Right?"

Gus starts looking for what he wants to take. Gladys excitedly says:

"Yeah, now, we get to, like, pick what we want."

"Only what *you* can carry...."

The Captain and Tennille

Early morning. Maude is out front of the Rodriguez house with her regular satchel and now a second, smaller, satchel. Gus comes out carrying his satchels and a plastic milk crate with five molotov cocktails in it. He sets the crate down and cups his now-free hands around his mouth.

"I'm gonna start pitching these bombs...at the count of ten!..."

Two scared young voices scream:

"*Wait!*"

Then.

"We're stuck!..."

"Come help us, Gus!"

Maude smirks. Gus shrugs and heads back into the house. After a moment he brings out the icon and sets it on the sidewalk on its stomach. Gus looks at the prone statue and then the two smaller kids.

"How you gonna carry this thing all over?"

"We can't leave it...."

"I'm not carrying it another meter."

Gus runs back in the house and comes out with the heavier of two crowbars. He strides up to the statue still face-down and before Walter or Gladys can say anything he swings and smacks the statue on the back of the neck. The head pops right off with a snap. Walter grabs Our Lady's head and turns it over. Her face is fine. Walter stands up cradling the head, he is crying. Gus is exasperated and says:

146

"You couldn't've taken the whole thing...."

"Look, Walter...we can carry the head in this bag."

Gladys wipes the head, shakes away loose plaster bits and then wraps it in a rectangle of plasticloth. Walter holds open the heavy plastic bag. Gladys manages to get the now padded head into the plastic bag.

Maude scrounges up some good-size stones. Gus points to the big picture window. Maude fastballs a stone, it hits the window hard. The pane fractures and falls away with a glorious crash. Gus lights one of the molotov cocktails, holds it a moment as the gas-soaked rag wick really gets going, and then he chucks it into the livingroom.

Maude moves down the length of the front of the house. She puts out one of the master bedroom windows. Gus is close behind with a gasoline bomb.

Gladys and Walter trail the arson duo to the back of the house. Gladys carrying the bag with the head in it and Walter their satchel. She nudges Walter with her elbow.

"See. And we can trade off carrying Her head. Right?"

"Yeah, Gladys. But, I.... You know...liked staying here...."

Gladys nods, but says:

"We need to get more serious about getting out...of America. Or at least Colorado. Before winter gets too bad."

Walter shrugs and complains.

"No one's gonna take us. They want doctors, and shit. Scientists.... People with money, you know."

Gladys starts to argue the point, but Walter cuts her off.

"There isn't, like, room...for all the people that want out...or, you know, got thrown out of places."

The fire in the Rodriguez house is really catching now. Flaring out through the already-broken windows. Other windows in the house are exploding and cracking.

Wind picks up snatches of flame and spreads the fire to a tree near the house. Then on to another tree, and so on.

The Ray Anthony Orchestra

Back on the MetroWeb. Things have gotten worse in just the couple weeks the kids were at the Rodriguezes. Fewer trains stopping in stations. Fewer and fewer stations still open.

The kids manage to squeeze aboard a string of freight cars that is being precariously dragged along the narrower commuter-gauge tracks by three old diesel engines. These engines billow long columns of black smoke. The four kids are sitting close together in a freight car full of people. Everyone is sitting down. Most are quiet. It is cold and damp.

There is no opportunity for crime.

The big metal door on one side of the freight car is slid wide open. The open doorway frames an industrial slum passing by fast in the gray morning light. Maude looks around and says:

"It was a stupid idea, us trying to go back south. UNNAA is too busy evacuating to feed us...."

"Whatever, Maude. You wanna walk?"

"I could get us a car.... With my new...credit card."

Gus scowls at the mention of the small square plastimetallic semiautomatic pistol Maude now has with her.

Gladys and Walter are sitting between Maude and Gus for warmth. Walter pipes up with:

"I rode in a limo, once."

No one acknowledges him. Walter continues, but on a different thought.

"With Maude's…thing…we could get a big car…and drive down south into Mexico. Join the Zapatas."

Gus scoffs.

"Za–pa–tis–tas."

Maude says:

"They're already up here. And they don't need much in the way of little boys in girl's clothes."

Gus laughs to himself. The train starts slowing down. Most people in the car stand up. A few of those who do not stand up are dead. A few are so sick or injured only their companions' efforts get them on their feet. The train grinds to a halt on siding tracks between stations.

After a few minutes everyone gets out of the freight cars. A few Canadian (white and native american) and Soviet (mostly white, a few central asian) Red Cross workers, and a small squad of Japanese Blue Helmets hand around material the UN wasn't going to have time to ship out before they leave.

Gus, Maude and Walter stand way off to one side. Gladys moves up into the attention range of a caucasian female Soviet Red Cross official. The other kids watch the Red Cross woman give Gladys a couple ration packets and Gladys wolf them down. The woman gives her a cigarette. Gladys and the Red Cross official talk a few minutes. The Soviet woman gets caught up in some trouble at the distribution line and Gladys slips away.

Gladys walks over to her friends as she carefully snuffs out the cigarette butt and shrugs at her companions.

"She said UNNAA is, like, all outta here in two weeks."

Gus groans and says:

"Oh crap, only two weeks? We gotta find those Bulgarians."

Gladys says:

"She said the Bulgarians are only sponsoring resettlement in southern Sudan, or Afghanistan."

Now Maude groans and then she growls:

"Shit... Harsh."

Gus asks his partner:

"Where's...Sudan? Close to Mexico?..."

Maude shakes her head and sighs and answers:

"Not very."

Gladys rubs her stomach and says:

"I'm hungry...."

"We saw you eating the Red Cross food."

"I'm still hungry...."

"Shut-the-fuck-up."

Walter wonders aloud:

"I thought Japan was s'posed bring in all that food for Christmas?"

"Food from Japan for Christmas? Where the fuck did you get that idea?"

"I think I heard it on the radio...."

Maude and Gladys laugh. Gus says:

"In your fucking mind the Japanese are bringing food for Christmas, huh?"

"Fuck you, Gus. I heard it."

Hugo Winterhaler and His Orchestra

Gus stops and excitedly says:

"There's Stapleton. See? Over there."

Northeast, about five, ten kilometers away, a constant stream of heavy jet aircraft lifting off and landing.

"Christ, the Blue Helmets *are* in a hurry...."

"We have to get there....With a big wad of cash."

Maude nods.

"Cash'll get us on one of those jets. Right?"

Gus and Maude look at each other.

"We should've got off at Littleton."

"I didn't know that would be the last fucking stop 'til here!"

"C'mon, c'mon. Walk while you talk."

They walk for eight or so hours. Maude really drives them. The last couple hours Gus trades off carrying one of the youngest for a bit and then the other, to keep the group moving. The only rest is when the kids have to stop and let columns of soldiers and local militia pass by on intersecting roads.

The kids eventually come to MetroWeb tracks. They hope it is a B-line. On that hope they follow these tracks north. Passing slower displaced persons also walking this MetroWeb line.

The sun goes down beyond the white juts of the Rocky

Mountains. It is getting colder fast.

"Gus. Stop. I gotta put on some more clothes."

The kids move off the tracks and up the embankment into the bushes. Gus keeps an eye out. The other three hastily add on the last of their clothing. Maude puts out her arm for Walter to brace on as he pulls a pair of wool slacks on over his layers of tights and under his two skirts.

Not so far behind them, a ragtag commuter train comes rumbling up around a bend. The kids grab their possibles.

This train is packed and spilling out. Some of the cars are nothing but a charred frame on a chassis. On one passing car a group of passengers is forcefully ejecting another passenger. The unfortunate is thrown, head-first and screaming, out of the commuter car doorway. For whatever reason, the train noisily grinds to a near-halt, barely dragging itself along.

"C'mon. It's gotta be going north...."

The kids dash and tumble down the steep slope to the tracks. Gus nearly trips over the man that was thrown from the train.

The train cars right in front of them are already packed, end-to-end, wall-to-wall.

There are people on top and a few clinging to the sides of the cars. It is these hangers-on that those on foot target when fighting to get aboard. Keeping a grip on the train and fighting is not easy. One black woman has herself tied to an exterior ladder. A pistol in each hand she shoots all who approach her.

Another commuter car and another pass by, both packed with weary and worn refugees silently looking at the four youths.

Maude lifts Walter onto the stubby end-platform of the next car. Gus lifts Gladys on next to Walter. The younger kids step back. Gus jumps up. Maude grips Gus' arm and pulls herself on board the end-of-car platform.

153

Gus looks into what's left of the car behind them. Crammed with a hundred or so paramilitaries. Silent, mostly sleeping. No obvious factional emblems. Hard to say, best not to find out. Heavily armed adults in makeshift uniforms are definitely not-to-touch.

Gus turns and looks to the doorway of the car ahead of them. Three huge people pressed together in a wedge fill the doorway. Sealing off entry to the forward car.

The three big people are wrapped so heavily in clothes and coats and shawls that their gender is indeterminate. One of them on one end is caucasian, the person in the middle is black and the third, who is asleep on their feet, is so well wrapped their ethnicity is also cloaked. The three big people do not acknowledge the kids, nor do they look at each other. Gladys frowns and mutters.

"Great. We're stuck."

The kids huddle in front of the three big people.

A white paramilitary man comes to the end-door of that car and stare at the kids. Especially the girls.

"Let's see ID. All of you."

Simple request. Simple response. Hands reach into and come out of pockets nice and slow and friendly. Plastic bags with ID inside handed over.

"Got much money?"

"None."

The paramilitary returns all IDs except Gladys'. He stares at Gladys' set of brightly colored EU ID and at her. Maude sees this look. She reaches through pockets and layers for the pistol. Gus spots her move, and he reaches nice and slow behind her and touches her right elbow. Maude jerks slightly and glares for a fraction of a moment at Gus. Maude's gun hand withdraws open and empty and she rests both hands at her side.

Militia man flings the handful of Gladys' brightly colored EU documents out away from the train. There is a brief rainbow splatter of reflective colored plastic in the air. Gladys is very good and she doesn't show any emotion or say anything. The paramilitary growls:

"The Euros never issued those...to *you*...."

Gladys steps back and moves behind Gus. Two more militia (both white) come up to the doorway. They are carrying a large sheet of black plastic tarp. One of them says to the man questioning Gladys.

"C'mon, Alacran. Lieutenant wants this door covered over. He's cold."

The inquisitor shrugs and turns and walks back into the car. The paramilitaries seal the heavy black plastic over the doorway. The between-train platforms are now darker. But there is less wind pulling at them.

Gladys exhales and quietly says:

"God-fucking-damnit."

A few hours pass. Sometimes the crawling train picks up a little speed, but only for brief stretches. The three people squashed together in the doorway to the car ahead of the kids occasionally shift about. Turning this way and that. Never looking directly at the four youths.

One of the big people wedged in the doorway pokes the one in the middle and makes some vocalizations that are too deeply muffled by the layers of wraps for the kids to hear. The person in the middle pokes the person on the other end, who is still sleeping.

The standing sleeper grunts awake and yells incoherently. The middle person shoves the waking sleeper and again speaks their muffled message. This time the woken one nods acknowledgment. After a moment of groping in their coat the still drowsy person hands over a plastic bag filled

155

with unknown stuff to the middle person. That person hands it to the person on the other side.

That first person unties the knot in the plastic bag and pulls out numerous newspaper clippings, which they study carefully one-by-one.

Another hour or so passes. Gus and Maude sharpen and clean their daggers. The three people filling the door of the forward car are mindful of the rasp rasp rasp of spit stones against dagger blades. The train the kids are on lurches to the left, shifting onto a siding track to go around an even slower train.

Gus cautiously leans out from the small end platform so he can see on ahead. Many other passengers are doing the same thing.

Ahead is a shorter slower train. A pseudo-commuter train made of flatcars with plywood over plastic frames that are fastened to the flatcar beds. These ersatz commuter cars have no window panes in the windows and no doors in the doorways.

As the speedier train passes the slower, the kids can see that the other train is not nearly as full of people as the one they're on. Gus looks at Maude and she nods yes. Gladys and Walter have their stuff and are ready to cross over to the other train.

The traincar platform the four youths are on comes alongside makeshift platforms between one set of the ersatz passenger cars. Gus steps over onto the slower train. With two quick lifts he moves the younger two on over. At that moment, the train Maude is still on picks up speed and moves ahead, nearly out of reach. Gus panics. He reaches out as Maude is already stepping forward. For a moment they are not in synch. Maude tilts the wrong way. She grips Gus' left arm as she leaps and lands safe next to him. Gus holds her tight for a moment.

Gus leads into the car ahead. It is only half-full, most are snoozing. As they walk through the car the kids examine the other passengers. No good targets here.

The next car's floor is torn-up in large patches down the car's length. It takes the four kids some while to cross this car. Most of that time is spent convincing Walter he'll make it. The car after that, and the next one, are full of wounded and a few medicals. Passage is slow.

Gladys steals the wallet of a white man with bandages covering his face.

This train is juiced by crude wood and coal-fed generators set up on the two flatbed cars behind the locomotives. When the engineer accelerates the train billows black oily smoke. And the train is moving along fast enough that the acrid black smoke whips back and passes through the train cars.

The kids work their way up the length of the short train until they are in a car not so far back from the engine.

In this car there is a knot of old women (three caucasian, two black, one mixed-race and one hispanic) huddled along a makeshift bench against one wall.

One of the older women (mixed-race) is better-dressed than her companions. Better-dressed in that her clothes are obviously clean and pressed. Several of the other women hold bits of cloth and plastic to shield the better-dressed woman from the filth of the train smoke.

With Gus leading, the four kids walk past the old women, giving them the once-over. At the car's forward doorway he hesitates, and looks at his partner. Maude whispers:

"Yeah. Looks like it to me."

"Hands and feet only. Right, Maude?…"

"Yes, Gus. No gun."

The two older kids are on the flanks with Gladys and

Walter in between.

The old women see the four kids coming back. The better dressed woman sits up straight and prepares to address the kids. The other elderly women huddle closer to their leader.

The leader woman starts to talk, but Gus walks right up and punches her hard in the face. The other kids attack the grannies. Hitting, kicking, punching.

"Give us your money!"

"Money! Now!"

The elders scream and lurch with the impact of even Walter and Gladys' blows.

Gus stops and steps back, the others follow. The women are crying and moaning. The better-dressed woman has gone unconscious.

"We don't want to hurt you anymore."

Gus leans down toward the elderly hispanic woman directly in front of him. She is spitting out broken pieces of her upper plate. She looks up into Gus' angry driven eyes. The woman is so hurt and frightened, so helpless, that Gus isn't really keeping an eye on her. A trailing waft of smoke momentarily clouds the car. Gus does not see the woman in front of him take a narrow-gauge plastimetal rod, nearly a meter long, from inside her coat.

The train tilts some as it corners. Gus leans forward. This momentum, plus the lesser force of the hispanic senior pushing the needley shaft up, combine to drive the needle point of the alloy rod nearly eight centimeters deep into Gus' upper right chest.

Gus is surprised. He jerks back upright. This motion yanks the rod out of the old woman's hands. It has punctured through the upper edge of Gus' right lung. The rod extends at a slight upward angle from his chest, a quivering insectoid antenna.

Gus' three friends are frozen, eyes on him. He slowly draws the rod out of his chest. All four of the kids look at the entry hole in Gus' coat, a dark bloom of blood seeps out around the hole.

The woman who stabbed Gus is still looking up at him. Maude takes out the pistol and shoots that woman, twice. With the barrel of the revolver being so snubbed the pistol's report is loud and the flash blinding white.

Gus manages to croak:

"Put it away!"

Maude stuffs the gun back in her coat. The better-dressed woman is conscious again. She and the other grannies are silent. Walter is sobbing. Maude turns to him.

"Shut-the-fuck-up!"

Gus gingerly works his shoulder and chest muscles. He winces and cringes.

"Jesus…. I think…she stabbed my lung…."

Maude and Gladys stare at Gus' pale face and Gladys whispers:

"Are you…dying, Gus?…"

Gus is blinking and taking rapid shallow breaths. He rasps:

"Fuck you…."

Gladys kicks the leader woman. Gladys hits her again and spits on her. Walter is still crying.

"We got to get Gus off the train."

Gus drops the poison-tipped rod to the floor. He stuffs his left hand way under his coat and clothes to his skin. He grits his teeth with pain and his hand comes out bloody.

Gladys gets out a fairly clean white T-shirt from her satchel.

"Maude, reach up and stick this over the wound."

Maude obliges. Gus' hands hang down at his sides, a dull grimace of pain on his face.

"Gus, press this over the hole. Right?"

Gus swallows and nods.

"I can...still breathe...plenty."

Maude nods. Gus hesitantly adds:

"I think...it's alright...."

Maude frowns, doubtful. Gus turns to the old women.

"We wouldn't, like, kill you...."

None of the old women answer. Gus kicks the dead woman. Maude pulls at him.

The four kids slowly head up to the forward doorway and out onto the between-car platforms. Maude holds onto Gladys with her good hand. Gladys leans way out and looks at the upcoming terrain. The makeshift passenger train the kids are on is still poking along, just a little faster than a quick walk.

"There's an open place...in a couple minutes...."

"Gus, c'mon. Stand up."

Gus looks at Maude, he is afraid and confused.

"My...right shoulder and upper arm...are...sort of...going numb...."

Walter is stricken.

"What...do you mean, Gus?"

Maude asks:

"Can you, like, get off the train, Gus?"

Gus takes his left hand away from the wound and the hand has some blood on it. He wipes his bloody hand on his pants and then he flexes his left hand's grip and nods a little. His lips and eyes are firm, but Maude is not sure. She says:

"OK. Soon as we get to that clearing...you first Gladys. Then you help Walter."

As the train passes alongside a relatively clear patch of earth, Gladys hops off the makeshift end of the car. Gladys turns, Walter takes her hand and he jumps the meter and a

160

half to earth. Maude steps up to the edge.

"I'm gonna step off and just, like, walk along. You reach and brace on me and step off."

Gus nods and Maude steps off the crawling train. She walks fast along with the train. Gus grabs her left shoulder and big steps off.

The shock of pain from the jolt of his landing on earth nearly causes Gus to blackout. He takes a long slow breath.

"We got to walk now, Gus."

Gus nods and silently they trudge off through the garbage-strewn field toward a road in the near distance.

Mantovani and His Orchestra

Unfortunately, after walking away from the MetroWeb tracks, the road the four youths come to leads almost directly to a checkpoint. A checkpoint manned by Team Jesus.

The line to have papers checked is long and slow.

The kids are in front of a caucasian family and behind a group of seven people of different races, mostly caucasian. The people in front are standing close around a couple wheelbarrows of possessions.

After just a few minutes in line Gus has to sit down. An african american man among the group in front of the four kids sees Gus is not doing well; keeping one hand pressed under his coat and close to falling as he sits down on the ground. The man watches Maude switch the now bloodied T-shirt with another T-shirt. He speaks to a companion and then comes over to the kids. Maude stands and stares at him, her pistol in hand in her coat pocket. The man stops and holds out his open hands.

"I'm a nurse...."

Maude looks at the man and then her ailing partner. The african american nurse looks at Maude for permission to examine Gus more closely. Maude scowls, and curtly nods.

The nurse crouches and sets a small plastic bag at his side. He quietly asks:

"Shot?..."

Maude glances around, crouches near the nurse and says:

"Stabbed."

"Shoulder?"

"Upper chest…."

"When?…"

"Maybe…a half-hour…."

The nurse speaks to Gus.

"Hey, chief."

Gus raises his head and tries to scrutinize the man crouched next to him. The nurse says:

"Buddy? Can you…move your arm?"

Gus painfully does so.

"Deep breath?"

Gus just shakes his head negatively.

"Still bleeding?"

"A little."

Gladys leans down toward the african american nurse.

"This old woman…."

Maude's hand sweeps out and slaps Gladys, hard. Gladys swings back at Maude, who easily parries. Gladys steps back, glares at Maude. Well out of Maude's reach, Walter loudly whispers:

"A pointy metal rod…."

Touching the red slap mark on her face, Gladys scowls at Maude and says to the nurse.

"Maybe in his lung…."

The nurse asks Gus:

"Coughing blood?"

Gus vigorously shakes his head no.

Maude mutters:

"He said…he's like…all numb in his chest and shoulder…and right arm…."

The nurse gets up and goes back to his chums around the wheelbarrows. He returns with a paper sack with food grease spots on it. Gladys and Walter stare at the bag.

"Here's some bread. Why don't you guys move up with us. After we get through I can look closer at your friend...."

Maude starts to agree.

Gus suddenly stands up. For a moment he teeters a bit. Gus looks down at the nurse, at the nurse's companions and then at his girlfriend. He tries to sound like he is in command when he says:

"No...."

Maude answers just as firmly:

"Let's go through the line with them, Gus. It'll be safer...."

Gus glares at the nurse.

"Are you...Secret Rapture?...".

The nurse shakes his head no.

Gus suddenly has to sit back down. Maude looks at the Team Jesus troops manning the roadblock with their tight minds and machineguns. Gus asks the question on her mind.

"How are we gonna get past *them*?"

The nurse smiles, raises his brow a moment and shrugs. Maude stares at him and shrugs.

"Gus.... Gus, listen to me. We don't have any choice...with you being sick...."

Gladys and Walter move right up and take the bag of bread from the nurse. He comes around to the other side of Gus.

"Can I give you a couple dermals? One for the pain, one to keep you conscious...."

Gus nods dully, now completely lost in his misery. The nurse peels the foil back off a low-dose heroin dermal and sticks it right on Gus' throat over one of the big veins. In but a moment Gus sags a bit. The nurse adds a couple other dermals onto Gus' upper arm, one of these is amphetamine. And the next moment Gus sits up and sort of shakes himself and

164

looks up and now he has some (chemically induced) life back in his eyes.

The nurse and Maude help Gus move up with the others and get him settled. One of the nurse's companions (native american) smiles at the kids.

"Just keep up with Nursie. We'll be home in a little while."

Gladys and Walter are chewing on bread and keeping one eye on the strangers and one eye on Gus. Gus is sitting on a plastic box set out for him. He looks better after the drugs. Alert and paying attention.

One of the other people in the group nudges the nurse. The nurse and Maude get Gus to his feet. Casually, the knot of people the kids are with shifts from in line to the edge of the road.

Up ahead there is a small explosion, and then two more, and then some shooting. Then smoke and yelling and screaming and more gunfire.

Maude reaches for her gun, but is interrupted by the nurse.

"C'mon. Move him. Now."

The kids and the seven adults melt off toward the big trucks Team Jesus rode in on. Two adults help Gus along. Most of the paramilitaries have run off to the situation.

At one of the big trucks there are three Team Jesus stormtroopers (all white) leaning against the truck and smoking cigarettes. One of these paramilitaries casually salutes the approaching group. Gus stumbles back trying to get free of the adults. Maude freezes and reaches for her pistol.

"What is this shit!?"

The nurse tries to reassure her.

"Look, you guys walked into a plan already underway."

Maude glares. Pistol out and gripped in front of her.

The other adults are not too interested in Maude's worries, and are getting into the back of the big canopy-covered truck bed. The nurse is irritated.

"They're with us, get it?"

"Fuck you."

Now everyone but the kids and the nurse is on board. The truck's engine starts up. Now the nurse is anxious.

"You guys got to get in *now*. Or get away from here fast…."

Gus grunts and pushes Maude aside and he tries to lift himself into the dark interior of the truck with his good arm. Maude gives up, pockets the gun and tries to help Gus. One of the other adults (hispanic) gets out of the truck to help the nurse with Gus.

The backdoor is shut even as they get Gus settled in the truck. One of the adults pounds on the wall behind the truck cab. The engine revs and they take off. Within minutes they are moving at a steady, rapid speed on some highway headed somewhere.

Maude is scared and determined. One hand inside her coat gripping the pistol. She wishes she had reloaded after shooting the old woman on the train. The nurse says to Walter.

"Hold this flashlight for me…. Thanks."

"Sit down. It'll be a half-hour until we get to where you're going."

Maude can sort of see the white woman who spoke. She is sitting on a plastic suitcase and holding out a package of cigarettes. Gladys reaches out, takes the cigarette pack, shakes out four cigarettes and hands back the pack. Maude lights the cigarettes one at a time. She gives the first lit to the now semiconscious Gus. Someone in the dark truck says:

"Christ. All four of you gotta smoke at the same time?!"

"Fuck you…. Right?"

All along the nurse has been cleaning and tending Gus' wound. Walter keeps the light beam as steady as he can. The nurse patches another heroin dermal to Gus' neck.

Henry Mancini and the Mancini Pops Orchestra

In about an hour the truck has made three stops and most of the passengers have slipped out into the early-evening.

The truck finally pulls off the highway into a vast barren complex of warehouses and mostly empty parkinglots. The truck the four kids and their hosts are in weaves through a series of traffic channels and tunnels and ramps. The truck pulls up to a secluded loading dock.

The backdoor of the truck opens and the nurse stands and helps Maude with Gus. It's when Maude is busy helping Gus that she feels most vulnerable.

There is a small open-faced wagon on four big hard-rubber wheels. They help Gus sit on it. He is just able to lie on the cart if he has his knees up and his feet resting on the edge of the cart. Two adults drag the cart. Low crunching rumble of the cart's wheels.

A vast empty warehouse. The small group heads down a wide dark hall to a freight elevator, which takes them up four floors. Then down another large dimly lit hall. There are windows in this hallway that look down over empty asphalt parkinglots.

The nurse unlocks a door. The wall lamp in the hall above the doorway casts some little light inside. Beyond that glimmer there is only darkness. The resounding echo of the nurse's entry steps suggest another huge empty warehouse space.

"Wait a second."

168

The nurse and one of the native american women go on into the dark space. After a few moments their footsteps stop and lights come on inside.

A second set of doors open into an even vaster warehouse. This superwarehouse is filled with several hundred rows of multi-story tiers of shelving that stretch to both ends of the space, perhaps a kilometer or more. These rows are broken up by intersecting causeways wide enough for two trucks to pass. All of it empty. Empty but for dust. Tinny metallic echo. Big clusters of neon lights dangling in rows from a metal frame suspended down to about 50 or so meters above the floor.

The nurse turns and points way across the length of the vast building at the distant 15-story high wall. He points to a long, long flight of narrow switchback steps that end, seven floors up that wall, at a small landing with a door and window.

"You four can stay up there...awhile."

They continue dragging Gus on the cart down a causeway between infinite rows of empty shelving.

"We sent for a doctor.... He works for us...."

They eventually make it to the seven-story staircase. Gladys and Walter look up it and groan.

The trip up is arduous, even with three adults essentially toting Gus. But the office space, long ago converted to a cubby-hole apartment, is warm and there is more food.

Maude and the nurse help Gus out of most of his clothes and then ease him down onto a narrow cot. Gus cannot move most of his upper right torso or arm. He shivers and his breathing is rapid and shallow. They pull a blanket up to his sternum.

The blood around Gus' wound has clotted and the T-shirt used as a bandage is stuck to the wound area. Maude and the nurse use warm water and gently pry it all loose.

Gus jerks and moans through clenched teeth.

The entrance wound is easy to spot. There is a four centimeter aureole of bright red blistered skin around the puncture site. The nurse stares at it. He slaps a couple more low-dosage heroin dermals on Gus' throat, waits a moment, and gingerly cleans and applies basic antibiotic bandages to the wound. Gladys and Walter are holding hands, standing near Gus. Gladys says:

"He, like, really needs a doctor, Maude."

Maude turns to the nurse.

"You said there was a doctor. Right?"

"He's on the way."

Maude stands up and walks to the window of the room. It looks out over the enormous enclosed space. Endless rows of empty shelving. Down on the warehouse floor, not too far from the base of the stairs, but screened from ground-floor view by a couple rows of the multi-floor shelving, there are several tables and pallets. Some of the pallets have sealed barrels on them, a few have stacks of large square plastic containers, rolls of black plastic and big rolls of black tape. There are signs of recent work.

Gladys asks the nurse.

"Can I, like, have one of your cigarettes?"

"Sure."

The nurse hands over his pack of cigarettes to Gladys. She takes one and hands them back. The nurse says:

"Keep 'em."

"Thanks."

Maude turns back to the nurse.

"Are you guys secret police?… One of the factions?…"

"No and no."

"You're not a fucking nurse. Right?"

"I've been a Nurse Practitioner for more years then you've been alive."

170

Maude ignores that and presses her main point.

"You guys gotta be…some sorta players. Right?"

The nurse shrugs off her question.

Maude looks back out the window down at the work area.

"I need some more bullets…for our gun…."

The nurse frowns. Gladys pipes up.

"I need, like, a whole new set of ID. EU…or like that."

The nurse shrugs. Gladys frowns.

Down across the warehouse, a big metal door opens. Light from beyond casts a brief long slender ray inward before the heavy door slams shut. The nurse snuffs out his cigarette and smiles a little bit, really more to himself.

"That'll be the doctor…."

It takes the doctor (older white man) nearly 45 minutes to work his way up the long switchback set of stairs to the small seventh-story room. Once he makes it to the top he leans heavily on the landing rail for support and takes long deep breaths. The doctor is wearing an expensive dark wool topcoat and carrying an opaque plastic valise.

The doctor does not even look at the nurse or the kids as he finally enters the room. He stands in the middle of the room and sets down his case. He has his eyes closed, still trying to catch his breath.

The old man finally looks at Gladys and Maude and then Walter. He pauses a single beat on Walter, then he lights a cigarette and looks at the nurse.

"I am not contracted…for this…kind of shit…."

The nurse stares at the cranky old white man and then quietly says:

"You are not fucking *contracted*…for anything, doctor."

The doctor frowns and looks away. The nurse smiles a little.

"That's right, buzzard. We call, and with no comment, or bitchiness...you show up and do the work....Yes or no?"

The old man subtly glowers and then gives the kids a second quick look.

"I am not a pediatrician.... But, they look fine....What am I to do?"

He smirks.

"Dose them for worms?..."

Maude lunges at the doctor and points.

"Him...asshole."

The doctor turns and looks at Gus. He takes off his top-coat and walks to Gus' side. He carefully lifts away the gauze resting on the puncture site. After five minutes of examination the doctor steps back and stands there thinking. His slightly glassy eyes focused on thoughts. Then he turns to the nurse.

"You're lucky...."

He scoffs.

"It's probably one of the crystallite poisons. But it is not Arrbaline or Debofatal.... He'd already be dead if it was."

A sickly smile.

"I cannot be accurate enough to say I can save his life.... I will try a few things."

The doctor shrugs noncommittally. In that moment Maude takes out her pistol and points it at the old white man's head. The doctor's pupils, constantly pinned, bounce wide with fear.

"I cannot work with this fat little bitch pointing a gun at me."

The nurse is smiling.

"You want *me* to point it at you instead? She won't shoot you unless I give the nod. Right, Maude?"

Maude ignores the amused nurse. Maude growls. The doctor sniffs and says:

172

"Alright. Let me get started then. I need electricity."

The doctor gets two antitoxin and two heroin dermal patches out of his bag. He applies the two antitoxins and one of the heroins to Gus. The doctor then pulls up his own right suit sleeve, unbuttons his shirt cuff and slides his shirt far enough up his arm to expose a used heroin dermal attached to his forearm. He removes the empty and applies the fresh heroin dermal. By the time he readjusts his clothing the patch is flowing into his system. The doctor's eyes close for half-a-moment longer than is normal.

He takes out two small intricate metallic devices that he delicately and firmly fastens with clamps and suction to Gus' chest over the wound site and then to each other. The devices form a seal over the puncture. Lastly he attaches an AC cord to one of the devices and hands the other end of the cord to the nurse.

"Plug it in."

There is an electrical outlet in the light fixture that hangs from the room's ceiling.

The doctor looks at a hand deck, and then he inputs commands. The machines begin probing Gus' chest tissue in and around the wound site. As the two machines interact with each other and with Gus' flesh, they whir and click and hum and emit periodic cooing hoots.

The doctor watches the hand deck's LCD a moment or two longer, and then sets the deck down on the table.

"This will take awhile."

The doctor looks at the other kids and then at the nurse. His lips barely crease into an ever-so-slight smile.

"Why don't I...put them all to sleep?... I mean...just for awhile...."

"Not me."

Maude steps away from the croaker and so does Gladys.

173

Walter pipes up.

"I need, like, something.... For my pain...."

The doctor slowly turns to Walter. Again the slight twist of his thin line of lips—could be a smile, could be a sneer.

"Pain?"

Walter is sitting on the edge of the desk, kicking his legs.

"All over."

"All over?"

Walter nods eagerly.

"But, like, don't make it too much.... I'll, you know, throw up."

The doctor smiles coldly.

"I'll take care of you...girlie."

Walter blushes. The old man unwraps a lowest-dosage heroin dermal patch and applies it to Walter's slender boyish throat, right over a main vein. In a moment Walter's face slackens. The doctor slides a hand down Walter's backside. He looks at the girls.

"You sure...you ladies aren't interested?"

Maude and Gladys are both firm in their nos. The doctor shrugs indifferently. Walter is curled into a comfy fetal ball on the desktop.

"Put the girlina out of my way some where."

The nurse carries Walter to an old overstuffed chair.

The doctor smokes expensive cigarettes and periodically consults his hand deck, occasionally adjusting the calibration of the machinery secured to Gus' wound. The pitch and tempo of the machines' noises alter in response.

Maude's attention is caught up by the big door across the warehouse opening and slamming closed a couple times. A half-dozen or so people eventually make their way across

174

the floor to the pallets and tables that are there to one side of the foot of the stairs. Maude watches these people set to work assembling the squarish objects that are eventually wrapped in black plastic and stored in the lidded containers.

A short while after the constructor crew leaves a second crew arrives. They pick certain of the black plastic–wrapped squares from inside the containers and take these objects away.

The doctor dismantles the apparatus affixed to Gus' injury. He seals both mechanisms into a thick yellow plastic bag, toxic waste emblem emblazoned on it.

"OK. I dissolved the toxin crystals. The pain and numbness will dissipate in a few days. He shouldn't use that arm much...for a week or two...at least."

The doctor purses his lips.

"No heavy lifting. Don't strain that lung. It'll rupture the plastiderm I pasted in down there."

When the doctor has all his stuff put away he fastens up his coat, and without looking at the nurse or the kids, he strides out the door, and slowly descends the stairs.

Now the nurse prepares to leave. He gestures at the room and at now sleeping Gus.

"This is all I can do for you guys. Like I said, you can stay here a few days."

The nurse points at the door and the stairs beyond.

"I won't be around. So, you want something...wait 'til you see someone downstairs and yell down to them."

The nurse buttons up his outer coat and says:

"Through that door...."

He points behind Maude at a door partly hidden by a multitude of coats hanging from a row of hooks along that wall.

175

"There's a little hall; at the end, on the left, is a bathroom. Sort of a shower in there too."

The nurse smiles and then leaves. Gladys watches him go and then looks over at the reposing Gus and then around the room. It's inside, it's warm and quiet. And Gus is too sick for him and Maude to fuck. Gladys smiles to herself and then wonders out loud:

"What are we going to do now?"

Maude looks at Gus and shrugs.

"Let's take showers."

Gladys brightens up.

"We can wash our clothes!"

The coats hanging on all those many pegs on the wall are mostly heavy rubberized coats with labels warning about proper contaminated clothing disposal. There are over a dozen of the coats. The two girls pile them on the floor. The uncovered door has no lock. It opens easily.

The hall is dark and less than two meters wide. Maude leans into the hall and searches the wall on both sides near the door. No light switch. A couple careful waves of an extended arm; nothing. Maude goes over to one of Gus' satchels and digs out his flashlight.

It is a short hall, three meters plus a bit. The hall ends in a large window of two panes, one above the other, in old wood frames that are faded, peeling and rickety. The lower of which slides up and down. More or less.

Cold winds rush in and the window frames rattle with each icy gust. The lower window frame is not pulled the last little bit all the way down and the clasp is not fastened that locks the two frames together in place.

The girls stand there peering out the window at the snow-covered fire escape landing just outside. A big gust of cold whooshes by the girl's faces. Maude frowns, reaches up and pulls down hard so the lower window frame is all the way closed. She twists the window clasp so it is locked shut. The window rattles less and is less drafty that way.

Outside, in the dark, it is still snowing. Snowflakes dash against the window glass. Dissolving in the middle of the panes and clinging in crystalline patches around the edges.

Maude points the flashlight beam out onto the fire escape landing. Metal stairs going up and down are visible, but beyond a meter or two the fire-escape is unseeable behind the snow and the night.

Maude swings the flashlight around to the door at her left. She opens this door. The room is very small. There is a toilet, a big plastic sink and four plastimetal sheets fastened into a tall box that is a shower stall. A nozzle, and knobs to control the water, hang from the ceiling. There is no light in the small room. There is a small opaque window high up on one wall, but nighttime renders it dark. Gladys says:

"I'm not, like, showering…in the dark…by myself."

"Yeah, yeah…. Walter needs a shower too. Right?"

"Leave me the flashlight."

"Sure."

Maude leaves the bathroom. Gladys hears her stride the short distance to the door at the other end of the hall, open it and close it behind her. Then there is silence.

The bathroom is cold and painted white. Gladys sweeps the flashlight beam along the walls. *666King* is scrawled with sloppy abandon at eye-level on one wall. Gladys opens the door to the hall, just a sliver, so if she peers just right, she can see most of the window and some of the snowy and dark form of the fire escape.

Gladys leaves the bathroom door ajar and starts to work her way out of enough layers of clothes so she can sit and pee.

Suddenly—urgent window rattling. Gladys hears a glass-muffled human voice cry out—scared and frustrated. From beyond the hall, outside on the fire escape.

Gladys is petrified with fear. No sound of Maude's return.

Rattle of the window. Frantic rattle of the window.

Gladys carefully scoots over to the slightly ajar door of the bathroom. Right up to the gap between the door and the door jam.

There is a young white boy out there on the fire escape. Driven panic on his face as he fumbles with the window that, suddenly, now for the first time, is not opening for him like it usually does.

Beside him, in the snow, on the fire escape, is a plasti-canvas bag filled with stuff he has stolen in his night's cat burgling.

The boy taps with both hands. Plaintive, muffled; Hey, hey.

No one comes to his aid.

All of a sudden, pounding down the fire escape from above, four or five big people in uniforms, logo of a major rentalcop corporation emblazoned big and bright on their chest. Their gender and race masked by the uniform face shields.

The young boy shrieks just once before a rentalcop stuffs three bulky leather-gloved fingers as deep into the boy's throat as they can go. Two other cops methodically and silently wail on the youth with their electro-batons. The thief convulses for a moment before he is frozen, stunned.

With brief, trained cutting, the rentalcops slice away the thief's boots and garments. Another rentalcop gags him and shackles the boy's ankles and wrists. One uniformed figure grabs the wrist chain and another the ankle set and they yank the boy half a meter off the frozen metal landing. He

178

jerks with pain. The rentalcops drop him into an opaque plastivinyl *Perp-Tote*™ and seal him in.

One rentalcop swings the *Perp-Tote*™ over a shoulder, another grabs the kid's bag of loot and all but one stride up the stairs, out of sight.

The last rentalcop scrutinizes the window. They try to open it up. The faceless uniformed enforcer sweeps their flashlight beam around the hall on the other side of the window.

Gladys is frozen standing with her face near the slightly open door. She is afraid to blink. She prays that Maude doesn't suddenly come through the door at the other end of the hall.

The rentalcop again tries the window. They study the clasp where the two window frames meets to confirm that it is locked. Then they follow the others back up the stairs. The rumble of heavy boots on the metal fire escape fades into the night.

Even after the last rentalcop is gone Gladys is frozen. She unsteadily wipes the sweat that is tickling along her upper lip.

Gladys opens the bathroom door a little more. Suddenly, at the other end of the hall, Maude opens that door and comes into the hall and walks casually down the short hall like nothing and nobody. She pushes at the bathroom door, but Gladys is standing in the way of the door opening fully.

"Hey. It's me, Glad."

Gladys steps back a bit unsteady. Maude opens the door and looks at her.

"What is it?"

Gladys is sweaty, scared and she keeps looking at the window. Maude turns and they both look at the window.

Maude looks at Gladys. Gladys doesn't say anything. She walks to the window. Maude follows a pace behind.

Even without using the flashlight they can see the cutaway remains of the boy's clothes lying haphazard on the fire escape landing and the first few stairs going down.

Already snow settles over these objects. The scuffle marks disappear into the white.

Floyd Cramer

For about a couple days the four kids are content just being there. Persons unknown show up at all different times and work among the tables and pallets. Some construct square objects that are tightly wrapped in black plastic and carefully stacked in the lidded containers on the pallets. Other people come and carefully remove the square objects and take them out of the warehouse.

Walter is usually the one that goes out on the landing and yells down to people for food. Usually, in a while, people trek up the many stairs with a bag of food.

On a small shelf Gladys and Walter set out a nest of some clothes. Gladys lays a shiny blue metallic cloth scarf over that pile, and then, with due ceremony, they ensconce the Bashed-Off Head of Mary on the shiny blue cloth.

By the evening meal of the third day Gus is feeding himself. And then he walks down the short hall to the pisser and back.

"Damnit, this arm still hurts like fuck."

"You used all the dope patches."

"Shit."

Gus tries to raise both arms. His right arm, shoulder and upper chest still hurt.

"How's your breathing?"

Gus' expression shifts from fretful to happy.

"Nearly good."

Maude steps back and walks to the window.

"I'm gonna go downstairs. See what's they're doing…."

Gladys steps in closer to Maude and the window. They both look down at the occasional work area. Behind them Gus says:

"Careful…."

"I'm not taking any chances…."

Maude opens the door and walks out onto the landing. Maude listens and looks. No one. She quietly closes the door behind her.

Gus sits down on the cot.

"Keep an eye on her."

Walter and Gladys don't answer. They are already watching their friend's rapid descent to the floor far below.

Once she is on the ground Maude moves quickly among the tables and pallets and containers. She touches nothing.

When she returns upstairs Maude is huffing and puffing. She closes the office apartment door behind her.

Gus rouses himself and sits up some.

"What are they making?"

Maude considers her words.

"Some sort of machines."

Maude sits down next to Gus.

"Do you think you can travel?"

"What's going on down there?"

She shrugs.

"I'm not sure."

Gus looks questioningly at his partner. He sighs and says:

"You really think we should go?… I guess I can try…."

He can't hide the disappointment in his voice. Maude nods yes. Gladys whines:

"But, it's so cold…and snowy. We, like, don't really know where we are….Where a train might be."

182

They decide to leave during the daylight, it'll be a little easier for Gus. So the next morning, when a few people show up and work at making the black plastic-wrapped square objects, Walter goes out and yells down for more food. A white woman eventually brings them a plastic container of food scraps. The kids eat half and pack the rest.

When the four get out onto the fire escape from the bathroom hall it has stopped snowing. But there is plenty of snow and ice covering everything. The thief boy's boots and clothes are still there, frozen to the fire escape under some snow and ice.

All around them are other vast hypercapacity warehousing facilities. Almost all are dark and silent. They look down the fire escape. It's about ten floors down to the ground. The fire escape seems to descend into an area of pavement that appears enclosed on all sides with buildings. There is a door visible. But ten floors is too far and it's too cold to get down there and then find the door locked and no way out but back up the fire escape. The metal staircase tops out at the roof which is eight stories up. Gus looks at Maude and says:

"Up, for sure."

The youths wrap their hands as best they can with pieces of cloth, but near the roof the tips of three of Walter's left fingers slip out of their wraps and get stuck to the frozen metal railing. Gladys grips his stuck hand and keeps talking to Walter to keep him from panicking and ripping his fingers free. All four of them drool and spit their body-temp saliva on the rail around the fingers. Once the surface skin layer of Walter's finger thaws it hurts like hell. As soon as his hand is free Walter starts crying. They bandage his three finger tips enough so he can make it on up to the roof.

It takes them an hour to get up the icy eight stories of fire escape to the roof. They stand there at the top sweating. With the rooftop windchill soon they are shivering.

Maude looks around at the panorama. Denver proper is that way. From over there, above Stapleton, jets are coming and going, evacuating UNNAA personnel from Colorado. Retired President Mandela's offer to fly to Denver for further mediation has been ignored by the forces on the ground in Colorado.

Maude watches the snake of jet airliners descending and ascending in tandem. Gladys yanks at Maude's coat sleeve. Maude pushes her and says:

"OK, OK."

About ten meters behind them on the roof is a cinder-block shed. The entrance to the service stairs and elevator.

When they get close enough the kids can see *666King* is spray-painted on the door. *Zapata*, in bigger letters, is sprayed in green over the top of *666King*.

The door has no lock. Gus rests against the cinder-block structure and Maude cautiously opens its door. Darkness and the hum of distant machinery. Inside is a small landing with the service elevator to the left. Long, winding stairs run down through the building to the right of the elevator.

Maude shoves the metal door closed behind them. Even though the cinderblock room is unheated, they feel warmer out of the wind.

Gladys studies the elevator's control panel. Gladys takes out her cracker card and inserts it in the card slot next to the controls. The panel's internal workings come to life. Chirps and brrrps, then a beep, then silence. Gladys studies it and then punches one of the unmarked buttons. Low tone of machinery humming down the elevator shaft.

"It's coming...."

The elevator arrives. They all get in. Gladys inserts her cracker card in one of the card slots of the car's internal controls, then punches BASEMENT 4. The kids all relax.

Two, three, four floors go by. Then with no notice the

car stops at floor nine. The door slides aside. A caucasian man in a technician's jumpsuit, fingers over the keypad of his hand deck, is standing there waiting to get on.

Before the technician can press the security icon on the hand deck screen, with his left hand Gus grabs the man's jumpsuit just below his chin as Maude grabs Gus around the waist to brace him. Gus heaves hard and jerks the man off his feet. Choking and flailing, the man is slammed, face first, into the wall of the elevator. Gus yanks backward hard and the technician stumbles back. Another hard yank forward, and again the man's skull slams into the elevator wall. Gus releases, and the unconscious man slumps down. Maude lets go of Gus. They high-five.

"I thought you had this machine under control, Glad?"

"I just got us on going down...."

"Can you keep it from stopping anywhere else?"

"I don't know."

"Try."

The unconscious technician occasionally twitches and groans.

Gladys presses her thumb on the BASEMENT 4 button, and keeps it there.

"That's gonna do it?"

Gladys shrugs.

The elevator descends all the way without stopping. The kids bail out into the dimly lit sub-basement that is stuffy and very hot and filled with incredibly noisy air circulation equipment.

Gus and Maude use a length of electrical cord to secure the technician to a rail in the elevator. Gus finds a small metal bucket and sticks it so the elevator door can't close, and so it's out of reach of the now somewhat conscious technician.

Next to the elevator they just rode down is a big freight elevator. The kids get into the freight elevator. Gus swings

185

the gate door down. Maude keeps her hands pressed on the appropriate lever and the elevator slowly trundles upward. It makes an awful racket.

They ride this elevator up to EMPLOYEE FACILITIES, just below MAIN FLOOR. The elevator stops, the door slides open. Dimly lit back hall near an empty employee cafeteria.

The kids move low and fast following the green EXIT signs. They come to a door with a big sticker on it warning that opening this door will activate a fire alarm. Maude pushes the door open. No sound. Nothing.

This outer door opens to a side lot stacked with sundry equipment and surplus. Luckily, the snow is not too deep. Yet. They work their way through the snow and machinery to a chainlink fence. Maude gets their wire cutters out of Gus' main satchel and snips a hole in the fence.

Beyond the fence is a field, and beyond the field is a road. That road intersects a bigger arterial. At this intersection they stop beside a wall to rest, especially Gus.

"Let me see your compass, Gus."

"It's in this pocket...over here."

Maude reaches inside a flap of coat lining and finds their semi-functional compass. She flips open the lid. After a moment to let the directional needle settle, Gladys lights a match and cups the flame with her hand. Both to direct its weak light and to shield the tiny flame from some of the wind. Maude turns slowly so she is facing southeast.

"All right. That's toward Stapleton, and whatever Blue Helmets are left in Colorado."

Barbra Streisand

The four kids trudge along, huddled as close as they can to one another. Trying to reduce exposure to the wind. They walk and rest and walk. The food they brought with them from the warehouse is finished off.

"The more...you chew your food, Walter...the longer it lasts in your stomach.... And the more good it does for you...."

As darkness settles in, the wind drops away and low clouds insulate the earth a little.

Gladys spots a B-line sign. A dozen or more blocks beyond that they finally come to a MetroWeb station. The station's ex-parkinglot is piled with refugees and camp fires. It takes the kids nearly an hour to worm their way through the crowd outside.

Inside the station there are even more people. All waiting for a train. The gold, blue and green banner proclaiming the presence of a Golden West Guard unit flaps from the station's bent flagpole. Several of the soldiers are on the station's roof scouting for trains.

No train comes for several hours. The kids barter away more than they should to stand near a big fire. Walter and Gladys set out a small sheet of plastic for Gus to sit on.

Deep in the night one of the scouts yells down to his compatriots and the activity among the Westerners wakens the kids and the other refugees.

It is a short train, moving very slowly. The kids advance

to the edge of the platform. When the train is only a couple dozen meters distant Maude grabs Gus and yells to her friends.

"C'mon! Other side of the train."

She jumps down. Gus puts out his good arm and takes Maude's extended hand and he jumps down. Gladys jumps right after him and then Walter. Gladys hits the uneven rocky bed below and topples over and squeaks. Gus grabs her and tosses her to the other side of the tracks, toward where Walter has already scurried.

The train slowly rumbles forward. A few other displaced persons have abandoned the platform for this side of the tracks as well. The four kids look for an opening to board. It'll have to be soon, the train is short and the mob on the platform is already rushing it.

"Here."

Maude grabs a rail and jumps up on an end-of-car platform.

"Glad, Walter. C'mon."

The two youngest run along with the slowing train. Maude yanks up Walter and then Gladys. Gus is last and he reaches up and grabs a railing with his left hand and leaps on board.

The train has barely stopped in the station before the crowd surges forward. It takes fifteen minutes for the conductors (mostly white) and their hired guns (a mix of races) to regain control of the train. It pulls out as slowly as it rolled in.

"Listen."

Gus says low and confident to Maude.

"If you see someone...tasty looking.... I could be into taking them."

"You're not ready to strong arm...."

"I could do it. You'd be right in there…taking up the slack."

"When haven't I?…"

Maude frowns. Gus makes a show of stretching his right arm in a series of moves that a few days ago he couldn't have done. Maude shrugs.

"Look…everyone on the trains ain't a…helpless trixie. We could pick 'em wrong…."

Gus is angry.

"There's no UNNAA handing around food, Maude…. We gotta take care of ourselves…."

"Yeah…and taking care…is not about you, crippled, trying to rob somebody…."

"You think Walter's right? That the Japanese are bringing Christmas presents?!"

Walter butts in.

"I said food…."

Gus shakes his head. Maude's answer to all this is:

"It'd be easier if I used my new tool…."

"No!"

The two older kids look like they are going to fight. Christ, Gladys thinks, they're not fucking enough. She smirks to herself, and then tries to diffuse the anger.

"I seen some Soviet Red Cross guys today. And you know the Soviets won't give up on…."

Gus angrily cuts her off.

"You're lying, bitch! I ain't seen a Soviet since before Lakewood."

Gladys sticks out her tongue at him and says:

"The Soviets won't abandon everyone…."

Gus scoffs. Gladys says:

"You just don't like Stalin."

"He's fucking dead! Dead….That Polish Red Cross guy was pulling your damn leg, Glad!…"

189

Gladys starts to rebut, Maude raises a fist and snarls.

"No! I do not want to hear any more shit...about is or is not Stalin dead. Right?"

Maude stares from one to the other. But Gus can't resist.

"Dead or fucking not...Stalin's not doing shit for us right here...."

Petula Clark

All morning this train has made several stops taking on more travelers and refugees. And now, once again, the train starts to slow, and shifts tracks into a station. Gus cautiously sticks his head out a broken window and looks up ahead at the oncoming station.

The train the kids are on has pulled off the mainline because there is another train stopped ahead on the through tracks. The train the four youths are on is presuming to bypass this blockage via the siding tracks through the station.

But there is a problem. The train eases into the station to find another train is stopped on those tracks too, blocking the way forward from the station. Steel wheels screeching to a stop.

The station platform seems empty, and yet functional, Gus turns and sees a dumpy elderly couple (male hispanic, female caucasian) trying to surreptitiously shift the hiding place of their roll of cash. Gus touches Maude's shoulder and directs her attention to his targets. Maude gets angry.

"No, Gus."

Gus ignores her and heads to the old people. The seniors see Gus coming. Maude rushes past him. When she gets right up to the old couple Maude pulls out her pistol. Gus tries to reach for the pistol as he says:

"Damnit, I told you…."

On the other side of the car, behind the kids, some people scream. They are not screaming because of the crime being attempted by the girl with a handgun.

The train the kids are on is now alongside the stalled train on the mainline that caused the detour into the station in the first place.

The train on the mainline had, up to this moment, appeared empty. But now, more and more heavily armed people are popping up in the windows of that train. Gus stands tall enough above the crowd so that he can see over most heads. Gus' eyes bug out. Pirates. Hundreds of them (all races). Each pirate has a rectangle swath of black face-paint across their eyes, nose, upper lip, brow, cheek. Screams now in all the cars of the trapped and ambushed train. Gus shouts over the crowd's surging panic.

"C'mon!"

He grabs Gladys. Maude grabs Walter. Gus yells:

"Brace me."

Maude does and he one-two kicks out the remaining plexiglass panel in a window facing the station.

Gladys and Walter scramble up and dive out the window. One-handed Gus is momentarily stuck in the window. Maude shoves him, he tumbles out. The train shudders as it tries to reverse. Maude stumbles slightly. She starts climbing out. Someone grabs her from behind. Maude presses her pistol to the person and pulls the trigger. Freed, she catapults out of the commuter car.

The four kids are about the first off the train. But already another hundred heavily armed pirates (half are non-white) have swarmed out of camouflaged bunkers built into the station. These corsairs also have the black swath on their faces.

The kids have jumped from a car near the back of the train. They try and run to the nearest set of wide exit stairs. But the distance is too far.

The crowd fleeing the train now surges backward, away from the onslaught of machinegun fire and hacking and slashing. The kids are also driven back toward the tracks. They try to move up the length of cars, but pirates (mostly white) spill around both ends of the short commuter train. Blocking this last avenue of evasion.

Slaughter, slaughter everywhere, but not a drop to drink.

The train guards (mostly black and hispanic) and conductors (mostly white) use flamethrowers to try and drive the crowd and the pirates away from the train. The engineer tries to get the train out of the station. It lurches forward, stops, then lurches back and slams into a barricade the marauders have thrown up behind it.

Gus frantically tries to decide if the engineer is likely to get the train out, and if they should get back on.

Pirates charge the kids. Gripping her pistol in both hands Maude shoots one of them.

Gus height also makes him an easy target. A pair of pirates (one caucasian, one asian) aim at him. The white corsair shoots first. Maude sees her boyfriend get hit. She grabs at Gus as he falls. Now the asian american pirate shoots at Gus. The second round hits him and passes through him and hits Maude in her liver. She presses a hand to the wound in her lower side and does not look down at it.

A bullet tears though Gladys' stomach. She drops screaming to the edge of the platform. Her coat gets caught up in the train. She drops her and Walter's satchel. Walter screams and grabs for Gladys and then he grabs their satchel and clutches it tightly to his chest. The train twists Gladys and flips her over and drags her through the crowd. In another moment Gladys is dragged under the train. Walter's screeching agony is what you hear in the jumble of the carnage.

The path ahead of Maude is suddenly clear. She sees that she and Walter are not far from an exit. Maude grabs Walter and they run for it. Maude gritting her teeth as they zoom across the few meters to the steps and leap up them, several at a time. Shots ring out and rounds crash into the cement steps where a breath ago the two kids trod.

Connie Francis

Evening shadows at midday. Long blocks of commercial and light industrial buildings. Many boarded up. Some sacked and burned. At the end of a less-damaged block, right near the corner of a large faceless cement building, is a set of concrete steps going up to a big handleless metal service door. To the left of the stairs and door is a deep cement utility trough that runs all the way to the next corner.

Here is Maude's corpse, propped where she left it—sitting on the steps at the service entrance, her left shoulder and her weary head leaning against the railing. The big gray cement building looming up behind. Walter stands on the steps next to ex-Maude. He quietly weeps and shivers.

Snow falls. Distant sonic rumble and roar of jet bombers and their payloads. Maude has been sitting there dead long enough that snow has built up in a fine coat over her quickly cold body.

Walter sets down his and Gladys' satchel. Walter wearily leans back against the railing opposite Maude's corpse.

Blood is turning the snow red where Maude's dead body sits.

Walter had helped Maude up a couple of the wide steps, and then he helped her sit and rest herself. Maude was so tired by then. Walter helped her unbutton her coat. Blood had already darkened her clothes from her abdomen down into her lap. Maude looked at Walter, and gave the frightened boy a slight smile as she murmured:

"Gimme a second...."

And then Maude died.

Walter steps back and stares. Snow now nearly disguises Maude's upturned face. He gingerly searches a few of her pockets and then beneath a couple layers of her garments. He retrieves a variety of things. He examines and discards most them. Walter finds a creased snapshot of Gus and Maude. They are both smiling, standing with arms around each other's waists. It is sunny and they are in short-sleeved T-shirts. Walter pockets the photo. He wishes he had a photo of Gladys, but this will help.

Walter takes Maude's dagger out of its hidden scabbard in her coat's lining. With the dagger he cuts loose Maude's satchel from its straps around her shoulders.

Walter slings his and Gladys' possibles on his back and grips Maude's in his arms. He looks at the dagger, holding it out so snowflakes accumulate on the cold flat steel blade and then slides it back in Maude's coat sheath. He looks at Maude a last time. Walter turns and hurries, running away into the snowy night.

Walter's urgent booted trot across concrete and asphalt is quickly lost in the muffling snow.

In the utility trench there are a bunch of juncture boxes involving this building's ventilation and operating system. The junctures are securely bolted into a stack and bolted to the base of the concrete stairway Maude's corpse slumps on.

The juncture boxes buzz and hum.

Down on the cement floor of the utility trough, just in front of the several-meters-high stack of juncture boxes, are two of the square objects wrapped in heavy black plastic. These two presents sit, one on top of the other, with wires connecting them to each other.

Explosion rips the night. The blast fills everything you can see with smoke and falling debris. The blast echoes colder than the early-December snow.

THE COMPLETE SMART ART PRESS CATALOGUE

VOLUME III (Nos. 21-30)

VOLUME IV (Nos. 31- 40)

Smart Art Press · Bergamot Station · 2525 Michigan Avenue
Building C-1 · Santa Monica CA 90404
tel 310.264.4678 fax 310.264.4682
www.smartartpress.com

SEMIOTEXT(E) NATIVE AGENTS SERIES
Chris Kraus, Editor

SEMIOTEXT(E) · P.O. BOX 568, WILLIAMSBURGH STATION
BROOKLYN, NY 11211 · TEL/FAX 718.963.2603
INFO@SEMIOTEXTE.ORG · WWW.SEMIOTEXTE.ORG

SEMIOTEXT(E) FOREIGN AGENTS SERIES
Jim Fleming & Sylvère Lotringer, Editors

SEMIOTEXT(E) · P.O. BOX 568, WILLIAMSBURGH STATION
BROOKLYN, NY 11211 · TEL/FAX 718.963.2603
INFO@SEMIOTEXTE.ORG · WWW.SEMIOTEXTE.ORG

SEMIOTEXT(E) DOUBLE AGENTS SERIES
Jim Fleming & Sylvère Lotringer, Editors

SEMIOTEXT(E) · P.O. BOX 568, WILLIAMSBURGH STATION
BROOKLYN, NY 11211 · TEL/FAX 718.963.2603
INFO@SEMIOTEXTE.ORG · WWW.SEMIOTEXTE.ORG

SEMIOTEXT(E), THE JOURNAL
Jim Fleming & Sylvère Lotringer, Series Editors

Polysexuality *François Peraldi, ed.*	$12
Oasis *Timothy Maliqalim Simone et al., eds.*	$8
Semiotext(e) USA *Jim Fleming and Peter Lamborn Wilson, eds.*	$12
Semiotext(e) Architecture *Hraztan Zeitlian, ed.*	$15
Semiotext(e) SF *Rudy Rucker, Robert Anton Wilson, Peter Lamborn Wilson, eds.*	$12
Radiotext(e) *Neil Strauss and Dave Mandl, eds.*	$14
Semiotext(e) CANADAs *Jordan Zinovich, ed.*	$12
Imported: A Reading Seminar *Rainer Ganahl, ed.*	$14

SEMIOTEXT(E) · P.O. BOX 568, WILLIAMSBURGH STATION
BROOKLYN, NY 11211 · TEL/FAX 718.963.2603
INFO@SEMIOTEXTE.ORG · WWW.SEMIOTEXTE.ORG